Verse
by
Verse

A Devotional Commentary
on
1st, 2nd, & 3rd John

Verse by Verse

A Devotional Commentary

on

1st, 2nd, & 3rd John

by Dr. Ricky Gravley Jr.

Word of His Mouth Publishers
Mooresboro, NC

All Scripture quotations are taken from the **King James Version** of the Bible.

ISBN: 978-1-941039-64-9
Printed in the United States of America
© 2025 by Dr. Ricky Gravley

Word of His Mouth Publishers
Mooresboro, NC
www.wordofhismouth.com

Introduction

The devotionals in this book are a compilation of emails sent out every Monday morning on our church website. I entitled the book "Verse by Verse" because I would take one verse and write a short devotional from that verse every week. I did not write it in commentary form, but I would take a thought or phrase from the text and build upon it. I trust and pray that you will read something from each devotional that will help strengthen your Christian walk.

Devotional books have always inspired me to meditate more on His Word, and they have challenged me to examine the text more closely to find the little hidden gems within each verse. I hope this edition of Verse by Verse will benefit you as you read through the books of 1, 2, and 3 John.

Dedication

I dedicate this book to my oldest daughter, Noel Williams, who has always been a great blessing to me. I am very thankful for her love for Christ and her dedication as she follows her husband and seeks God's will for her life. I have observed her as a faithful wife to her husband and a loving mother to her children. She has brought great joy and laughter to our lives as her parents.

Noel, I love you dearly, and I am thankful that the Lord has blessed you and your family.

Table of Contents

1 John 1

1 That which was from the beginning, which we have heard, which we have seen with our eyes, which we have looked upon, and our hands have handled, of the Word of life;

2 (For the life was manifested, and we have seen it, and bear witness, and shew unto you that eternal life, which was with the Father, and was manifested unto us;)

3 That which we have seen and heard declare we unto you, that ye also may have fellowship with us: and truly our fellowship is with the Father, and with his Son Jesus Christ.

4 And these things write we unto you, that your joy may be full.

5 This then is the message which we have heard of him, and declare unto you, that God is light, and in him is no darkness at all.

6 If we say that we have fellowship with him, and walk in darkness, we lie, and do not the truth:

7 But if we walk in the light, as he is in the light, we have fellowship one with another, and the blood of Jesus Christ his Son cleanseth us from all sin.

8 If we say that we have no sin, we deceive ourselves, and the truth is not in us.

9 If we confess our sins, he is faithful and just to forgive us our sins, and to cleanse us from all unrighteousness.

10 If we say that we have not sinned, we make him a liar, and his word is not in us.

"A Personal Relationship"

1 John 1:1 – *"That which was from the beginning, which we have heard, which we have seen with our eyes, which we have looked upon, and our hands have handled, of the Word of life;"*

The three beginnings in the Bible are found in Genesis 1:1, John 1:1, and 1 John 1:1. Genesis emphasizes the Creator on the morning of Creation. John emphasizes the Creator in the manifestation of Christ. 1 John emphasizes the Creator through the message of a Christian.

John wants us to know that he and the other disciples had a personal relationship with the Word of Life. He mentions four intimate details in this verse concerning the kind of relationship he had with Jesus. First, he had heard His voice. Second, he had seen Him with his eyes. Third, he had studied His life. Fourth, he had felt His touch.

What kind of relationship do you have with the Word of Life? If you desire to hear His voice, then read His Word. If you want to see His face, then believe His Word. If you want to know more about His life, then study His Word. If you need to feel His touch, then live by His Word.

You and I can have that same personal relationship with Jesus through the Word of God. Jesus is the living Word, and the Bible is the written Word. Allow me to challenge you to spend more time with the Word of Life.

"A Manifested Life"

1 John 1:2 – *"(For the life was manifested, and we have seen it, and bear witness, and shew unto you that eternal life, which was with the Father, and was manifested unto us;)"*

The word used for manifest means "to shine," "to bring to light," or "to show plainly." The life of Christ shined as no other life had ever shown before. Jesus proved He could give physical life when He raised Jairus' daughter from the dead. He proved He could give spiritual life when He healed the man sick of the palsy and forgave him of his sins. He proved He could give eternal life when He dismissed His Spirit on the cross and then rose again three days later.

If we take all of the days recorded in the Gospels concerning the life of Christ, they total less than forty days. However, those days bring to light and plainly show us the Father. They allow us to see the love, mercy, and grace of God through the life of Jesus.

Just as we can see God through the manifested life of Jesus, the world needs to see God in our lives. As Christians, we need to live a manifested life. Our lives should reflect both the Father and the Son. We need to bear witness by our walk, our words, and our willingness to serve the Father. This is how Jesus lived. If less than forty days of our life were recorded, what would it manifest? What would it bring to light? What would it show plainly?

"A Personal Connection"

1 John 1:3 – *"That which we have seen and heard declare we unto you, that ye also may have fellowship with us: and truly our fellowship is with the Father, and with his Son Jesus Christ."*

This is the third time, in three verses, that John declares he has seen Jesus. The apostle is as enthused about sharing Jesus as he was about seeing Him. Every believer should have this same zeal, both to see and to share Jesus. He tells us why he wants to share Jesus in this verse. The reason is that Jesus gives believers a personal connection. He brings us together in fellowship with each other.

The word fellowship is mentioned two times in this verse. The first time it is mentioned, it has to do with a saintly fellowship. The second time it is mentioned, it has to do with a spiritual fellowship. When our relationship is right with the Father and the Son, it will be right with the brethren. When we get out of fellowship in the spiritual realm, we will get out of fellowship in the saintly realm.

If an individual does not have a personal connection with the Father and the Son, then they will not have a personal connection with the saints. Salvation is what brings us into the fold, into the family, and into the fellowship. What a wonderful connection with Him and through Him!

"The Joy of Knowing Jesus"

1 John 1:4 – *"And these things write we unto you, that your joy may be full."*

Our verse for today will cause us to reflect on the earlier verses we have studied. Here we see John has written with a specific purpose in mind. He wants believers to have the fullness of joy. The "things" he has written about in the preceding verses all pertain to Jesus. John had experienced the joy of knowing Jesus, and he wanted others to experience this same joy also.

The fullness of his joy was that he knew Jesus on a personal level. It is plain to see in verse one that he had put his faith in the Savior. This is how he heard His voice, saw His face and felt His touch. You can never know Jesus apart from putting your faith and trust in Him. John believed in Jesus, and this brought him joy.

The fullness of John's joy was also in the fact that he knew Jesus on a powerful level. He saw the manifestation of His life in verse two. John knew the joy of seeing His power on display. He saw Jesus perform miracles in the lives of people. He watched Him change their lives and give them joy. The power of Jesus brings joy to all who witness it.

Finally, the fullness of his joy is that he knew Jesus on a productive level. John knew that what he had experienced and received, others could as well. We can find the joy of knowing Jesus by sharing Him with others. Try sharing Jesus with someone today and see if it does not produce joy in your life.

"God Is Light"

1 John 1:5 – *"This then is the message which we have heard of him, and declare unto you, that God is light, and in him is no darkness at all."*

The light of God is seen in His world. On the first morning of Creation, God caused the light to shine out of darkness (Gen.1:3). When Jesus was on the cross, God turned the light out in this world for three hours. Because He created the light, He can control the light. He created the sun, the moon, and the stars that shine upon us. Creation is God's visible proof that He is light.

The light of God is seen in His Word. Psalm 119:130 says, "The entrance of thy words giveth light; it giveth understanding unto the simple." The light of God can be seen in the pages of His Word. The Bible drives the darkness out of our lives and allows us to see God clearly. Creation and the Bible declare that God is light.

The light of God is seen in His workers. Matthew 5:14 says, "Ye are the light of the world. A city that is set on an hill cannot be hid." The believer is also proof that God is light. The change that salvation makes in the hearts of men reveals this great truth. Once we have been changed, we have both the duty and the desire to declare God's light to others. Because the child of God has experienced the light, he can express it to all the world. John is illustrating this in our text. Note that in verse five you have a child of God (His worker), declaring the truth of God (His Word), that God is light (to all His world).

"Living a Lie"

1 John 1:6 – *"If we say that we have fellowship with him, and walk in darkness, we lie, and do not the truth:"*

The believer's words and walk should always be in sync with each other. A double standard has caused the world to lose respect for modern-day Christendom. Sinners have no confidence in churchgoers who sin and party on Saturday night, then want to sing and pray on Sunday morning. They see these individuals for who they really are. They are hypocrites trying to ease their consciences with a little religion. So, the world developed a saying for them, "Practice what you preach."

Even the world knows that fellowship with God brings you out of the darkness. They understand that light and darkness do not dwell together. The man, or woman, who thinks they can live in sin and still have fellowship with God, is fooling no one but themselves. Sin separates man from God.

I remind you that John is talking to saints, not sinners. He is also talking about fellowship, not relationship. While our relationship with God is secure, our fellowship can be hindered and even severed if we choose to walk in darkness. Darkness is anything that is displeasing to God.

We should also note the word "walk" speaks of continual action. Walking is more than a step. Walking shows the direction and will of the individual. No one accidentally walks. This involves the person's mind and will. When believers walk in darkness after being in the light of God and His Word, it is by their own will and logic. They may say they are in fellowship with God, but in reality, they are living a lie. Walking in darkness will break fellowship with our Father, and it will cause us to live a lie and detour us from the truth.

"Living in the Son-Light"

1 John 1:7 – *"But if we walk in the light, as he is in the light, we have fellowship one with another, and the blood of Jesus Christ his Son cleanseth us from all sin."*

The happiest life is not living in the sunlight of God's world but rather living in the Son-light of God's Word. John gives three precious treasures in this verse that believers find when walking in the light of His Word.

First, we find Christ in the light. When we walk in the light of His Word we experience the reality of His presence. We see Him working in our lives. We hear His voice speaking to our hearts. If you want to be closer to Him, draw away from the darkness that may be in your life. Separate yourselves from everything that Christ would not be pleased with. Christ will not be found in the dark alleys of sin but in the light of His Word.

Secondly, we find Christians in the light. Christians are drawn to the light. Jesus is the common denominator that brings us all together. We enjoy one another because we enjoy Him. This is what makes our fellowship so wonderful. Think about all of the people you would have never met, had you not become a Christian. God has placed us in His family and given us brothers and sisters in Christ to help strengthen and enrich our walk with Him.

Finally, we find cleansing in the light. A dark room doesn't look bad until the light is turned on. The light shines and reveals the dirt. The light of the Word of God does the same in our lives. Once the dirt of our sin is revealed, we have the promise of cleansing through the blood of Jesus. These are three great treasures that can only be found in the Son-light.

"Self-Deception"

1 John 1:8 – *"If we say that we have no sin, we deceive ourselves, and the truth is not in us."*

Today's world is filled with deceit. It all started in the Garden of Eden with the devil and Eve. A simple conversation casting doubt on the truth of God's Word caused a catastrophic reaction. Since that day, deception has infiltrated our society like cancer out of control. Truth has fallen in the streets! The world would rather believe a lie than know the truth about sin.

Self-deception defiles our speech. Keep in mind that John is talking to believers. It is shocking that anyone could reach a point where they believe they have no sin. What is more shocking is that they would be vocal about it. This proves that the heart always affects the tongue. Self-deception causes an individual to lie. It causes them to say things that are not true and that are contrary to the Word of God.

Self-deception displays our sinfulness. Man can become deceitful because man is sinful. Self-deception reveals how corrupt the heart of man really is. We have the capability of deceiving ourselves, all by ourselves. We can easily convince our flesh that what we are doing is okay when, in reality, it is not.

Self-deception denies the Scriptures. Have you ever heard someone take a passage out of context to try to justify their sin? Perhaps you have heard them say things like, "Well, that's your interpretation of the Bible." Or maybe, "I used to believe it that way, but now I see it differently." Sin will cause us to deny what God has stated clearly. Many today like to twist the Scriptures, take them out of context, or ignore them completely to continue in their sinful deeds. Do not listen to your flesh. Look into the Book and allow God to show you the truth of His Word.

"The Only Thing You Can Do"

1 John 1:9 – *"If we confess our sins, he is faithful and just to forgive us our sins, and to cleanse us from all unrighteousness."*

John has a lot to say about sin in this one verse. He first mentions the confession of sin. Secondly, he highlights the comfort of sin. Finally, he emphasizes the cleansing from all sin. As believers, we should note that there is a responsibility on our part and on the Lord's part to deal with our sin. However, there is only one thing you and I can do about our sin. We read this in the first part of the verse. Whenever we sin, all we can do is confess it before God. I want us to consider our part in this text.

This is a pivotal statement. This verse begins with the word "If," which is a conditional word. God will not act until we first decide what we are going to do about our sin. Whenever a believer chooses to hide his sin, God will then reprove and punish him. But, whenever a believer confesses his sin, God is ready to respond in mercy.

This is a personal statement. Each individual must be willing to confess their sins before God. It is very easy to point out the sins of others and not our own. God wants us to put the spotlight on our own sins, not the sins of others. He wants us to confess our sins daily before Him.

This is a practical statement. John is not asking us to do something that is beyond our capability. It's not that hard to confess our sins if we humble ourselves before God. Man can be so prideful that he would rather pay some form of penance rather than come clean and confess his sins. Forgiveness and cleansing are available if we will obey this verse. When we sin, confession is the only thing we can do to fix the situation. Confession is the only thing we have to do. God will do the rest.

"Owning Your Sin"

1 John 1:10 – "If we say that we have not sinned, we make him a liar, and his word is not in us."

God desires to fellowship with His children. He loves every one of us. He does not want sin to interrupt the closeness that we can have together with Him. Several verses in this chapter have emphasized us taking responsibility, confessing, and forsaking our sins. John has shown us the benefits and consequences of our actions when it comes to facing our sins.

This verse simply teaches us to take ownership in this matter. We should always be in agreement with God and the Bible when it comes to any subject, but especially this one. Denial of our sin, as we have already seen, leads to deception. Deception just leads to more disobedience.

Believers that are filled with the Spirit are constantly taking inventory of their lives. They know that each day they live in sinful flesh and a sinful world. They know that there are sins of omission and sins of commission. They know that if the Holy Spirit reveals something in their life that is displeasing to God, then they must take ownership of it.

To act as though we have no sin is a sin within itself. The first step to realizing that you need Christ is understanding that you are a sinner. You realize you have a sin nature, and that sin is ever-present. This does not change when we get saved but becomes more of a reality. Taking ownership of our sins and confessing them to God pleases the Father.

1 John 2

1 My little children, these things write I unto you, that ye sin not. And if any man sin, we have an advocate with the Father, Jesus Christ the righteous:

2 And he is the propitiation for our sins: and not for ours only, but also for the sins of the whole world.

3 And hereby we do know that we know him, if we keep his commandments.

4 He that saith, I know him, and keepeth not his commandments, is a liar, and the truth is not in him.

5 But whoso keepeth his word, in him verily is the love of God perfected: hereby know we that we are in him.

6 He that saith he abideth in him ought himself also so to walk, even as he walked.

7 Brethren, I write no new commandment unto you, but an old commandment which ye had from the beginning. The old commandment is the word which ye have heard from the beginning.

8 Again, a new commandment I write unto you, which thing is true in him and in you: because the darkness is past, and the true light now shineth.

9 He that saith he is in the light, and hateth his brother, is in darkness even until now.

10 He that loveth his brother abideth in the light, and there is none occasion of stumbling in him.

11 But he that hateth his brother is in darkness, and walketh in darkness, and knoweth not whither he goeth, because that darkness hath blinded his eyes.

12 I write unto you, little children, because your sins are forgiven you for his name's sake.

13 I write unto you, fathers, because ye have known him that is from the beginning. I write unto you, young men, because ye have overcome the wicked one. I write unto you, little children, because ye have known the Father.

14 I have written unto you, fathers, because ye have known him that is from the beginning. I have written unto you, young men, because ye are strong, and the word of God abideth in you, and ye have overcome the wicked one.

15 Love not the world, neither the things that are in the world. If any man love the world, the love of the Father is not in him.

16 For all that is in the world, the lust of the flesh, and the lust of the eyes, and the pride of life, is not of the Father, but is of the world.

17 And the world passeth away, and the lust thereof: but he that doeth the will of God abideth for ever.

18 Little children, it is the last time: and as ye have heard that antichrist shall come, even now are there many antichrists; whereby we know that it is the last time.

19 They went out from us, but they were not of us; for if they had been of us, they would no doubt have continued with us: but they went out, that they might be made manifest that they were not all of us.

20 But ye have an unction from the Holy One, and ye know all things.

21 I have not written unto you because ye know not the truth, but because ye know it, and that no lie is of the truth.

22 Who is a liar but he that denieth that Jesus is the Christ? He is antichrist, that denieth the Father and the Son.

23 Whosoever denieth the Son, the same hath not the Father: he that acknowledgeth the Son hath the Father also.

24 Let that therefore abide in you, which ye have heard from the beginning. If that which ye have heard from the beginning shall remain in you, ye also shall continue in the Son, and in the Father.

25 And this is the promise that he hath promised us, even eternal life.

26 These things have I written unto you concerning them that seduce you.

27 But the anointing which ye have received of him abideth in you, and ye need not that any man teach you: but as the same anointing teacheth you of all things, and is truth, and is no lie, and even as it hath taught you, ye shall abide in him.

28 And now, little children, abide in him; that, when he shall appear, we may have confidence, and not be ashamed before him at his coming.

29 If ye know that he is righteous, ye know that every one that doeth righteousness is born of him.

"We Have an Advocate"

1 John 2:1 – *"My little children, these things write I unto you, that ye sin not. And if any man sin, we have an advocate with the Father, Jesus Christ the righteous:"*

The word "advocate" means an individual who pleads for the cause of another. A good example of an advocate would be a lawyer in a courtroom. He is one who publicly supports or recommends a particular cause or policy. Our text declares that we as Christians have an advocate. We have someone who is willing to plead on our behalf. This is not just anyone, but our text declares that it's Jesus Christ the Righteous.

The same word for "advocate" in this verse is translated as "comforter" in John 14:16-17. What a joy to know that we have the Holy Spirit to help us on earth and Christ to help us in heaven. The Spirit of God guides us from sin, and Christ our Advocate is there to help us whenever we have sinned. God has given us every provision we need to live a life free from the bondage of sin.

In our previous devotionals, we learned that man at his best will sin. Even though we are saved, we are still sinners. We will continue to stumble and sin as long as we live in this sinful flesh. Knowing Christ is our Advocate gives us the strength to strive against sin. This is the admonition John gives us in this verse. Our goal should be not to sin. When we come short of this goal, we should remember there is hope. Our Advocate is there to plead our cause if we will confess and forsake our sin. We do not have to despair, because we have an Advocate.

"The Sins of the Whole World"

1 John 2:2 – *"And he is the propitiation for our sins: and not for ours only, but also for the sins of the whole world."*

Think for a moment about all the sins you have committed. The sins of omission and the sins of commission. They are more than you could ever recall, and these are just your past sins. Now think about your present sins. How many are there? They, too, are more than you can count. If you were to begin confessing them right now, it would take the Holy Spirit to bring them to light, so you could confess each one of them. Finally, consider the sins of your future. This is beyond our knowledge, for no individual knows how many sins he will commit during the remainder of his life. Remember, we are only talking about your sins, and your sins alone are an immeasurable amount.

Now, let's consider an earth-shaking number of sins. Let's pile the sins of the whole world on top of your sins. We are not just talking about the present world, but we are talking about the sins of all humanity. From Adam in the garden to the last individual that will be born, that will live, and that will die. This goes beyond our human comprehension. Only God could know every single sin of every single human that has, is, and will live upon this earth.

What's more overwhelming than our sins is the graciousness of our Savior! If He were only the propitiation for your sin, that would be impressive. But the fact that Christ could appease God for the sins of the whole world is glorious! His blood washes away every man's sin. Christ is the hope for every man of every race, creed, and color. He was the propitiation yesterday, He still is today, and He will be tomorrow. What a great verse, and what great truth to share with someone today!

"Assurance in Obedience"

1 John 2:3 – *"And hereby we do know that we know him, if we keep his commandments."*

The verse before us tells us how to know for sure if we truly know Him. I'm thankful that we have a Book that helps us to have this assurance. There are so many in the world who have never met Him. Then, some who have met Him have lost the assurance as to whether or not they really know Him. God wants us to live with the knowledge of our salvation. The knowledge of salvation brings us the assurance of our salvation. Even with all the confusion that is in the world today, the Bible makes this very simple.

Throughout the book of 1 John, we will come across verses that will give us instructions on how we can know if we truly know Him. John is bringing to light that believers cannot live in a right fellowship with God if they are not assured that they have a right relationship with God. There is a great difference between relationship and fellowship. Once a believer's relationship has been settled, and they know that they know Him, then they can fellowship with Him.

This assurance comes through obedience. The condition in our verse for having assurance is based on obedience. We are to learn His commandments and keep them. This means living a life of obedience. Obedient believers live in victory and faith. Disobedient believers live in doubt and confusion. Oftentimes, people doubt their salvation and lose their assurance because they have unconfessed sin in their lives. The more we obey Him, the closer we get to Him and the stronger our fellowship becomes with Him. It is very simple: obedience brings assurance, and assurance brings the knowledge that we know Him. Choose to live your life today in obedience to His Word.

"A False Witness"

1 John 2:4 – *"He that saith, I know him, and keepeth not his commandments, is a liar, and the truth is not in him."*

Many people profess to know Christ, but their lives say otherwise. They are good at talking the talk, but not walking the walk. This is not my judgment, nor the judgment of others, but it's just a simple fact. They are saying one thing, and their lives say another. The Scripture we read today calls them a liar. It goes even further to say that the truth is not in them. They are classified in our verse as false witnesses.

The world is filled with false witnesses. The Bible says that we know them because they do not keep His commandments. How many people do we know who say they are saved, yet they have no desire to please God in their daily lives? Christians have a desire to follow His commandments. We may fail God and even disobey Him at times in our lives; however, a true child of God is grieved when he sins. He is so grieved that he wants to make his relationship right with God and get back in obedience to His will. He cannot continue to live a lie and expect to have any joy or peace.

This is not true with false witnesses. They can continue living the lie. It does not bother them to profess their faith and continue in sin, because it's all empty words. Remember, just saying it does not make it so. Obedience to the commandments of the Scriptures reveals to the world what you really have. Disobedience to the commandments of the Scriptures reveals to the world what you do not have. Those who know the Truth also love the Truth and walk in the Truth. Does your life line up with the Truth? Does your life support your testimony? Being a witness for Christ is not just revealed in our talk, but it's revealed in our walk.

"Complete Love"

1 John 2:5 – "But whoso keepeth his word, in him verily is the love of God perfected: hereby know we that we are in him."

Romans 5:5 declares that when we are saved, "the love of God is shed abroad in our hearts." This is evidence of true salvation in our lives. Salvation produces a love for God and the things of God. Our spirit becomes alive in Christ, causing us to love the spiritual things of God. We love His Word, His Spirit, His church, and His will.

Like any relationship, love can grow stronger or weaker. I'm glad we have the assurance that His love is unconditional and unchanging. The love of God is complete. God cannot love us any more than He already does, and He will not love us any less. He proved His love for us at Calvary in giving His Son for us.

He desires our love to be complete as well. The word "perfected" in our verse means fully developed. For our love to grow and fully develop for God, we must keep His Word. Some will see this as a heavy burden or task. However, when you love someone, obedience is not nearly as difficult as it looks. I'm not saying that it's always easy to obey, but love always prevails and causes obedience. A child may not always want to obey his parents, but the more he loves them, the more he desires to obey them.

God gave us His Word to instruct us on how we ought to live. He wants us to draw closer to Him and obey Him because He loves us and wants the best for us. Obedience causes our lives to fully develop and gives us the assurance that we are in the right relationship with Him. It causes our lives to be complete. Purpose to obey Him, and allow your love to develop deeper for Him.

"Walk the Talk"

1 John 2:6 – *"He that saith he abideth in him ought himself also so to walk, even as he walked."*

The principle in our verse is very practical. An individual who professes to know Christ should walk as Christ walked. We should not just profess Christianity with our lips, but also with our lives. We should walk the talk. The world has no respect for an individual who only praises Christ with their vocabulary. The world is spiritually blind and walks by sight. They need to see us walking in the footsteps of our Savior.

The keyword in our verse is "abide." A carnal believer has no effect on the world because he is not abiding in the presence of Christ. When we abide in Him, He changes our lives drastically. He changes our speech, manner of dress, the crowd we run with, our desires, and many other things about us. Abiding Christians have a different focus on life. They have inward joy and peace beyond understanding. This creates an even greater hunger to walk as He walks. We understand the riches of a personal relationship with the Lord.

Abiding in Christ is what gives us the ability to walk the talk. There is no way we can do this in our own power and strength. We must have His help in our lives to walk as He commands us to. There is no struggle when we abide in Him. Walking the walk can be as simple as talking the talk when it is done in the power of the Spirit, rather than the energy of our flesh. The answer is to abide. Let Christ's Word do the leading, you and I do the following, and our lives do the talking. This will cause the world to take note of what salvation can do in us and through us. Make it your goal today to walk the talk.

"I'll Take the Old Book"

1 John 2:7 – "Brethren, I write no new commandment unto you, but an old commandment which ye had from the beginning. The old commandment is the word which ye have heard from the beginning."

John was not trying to write something new and improved, but rather he takes believers back to the Word of God. He reminds them of the words of Jesus in John 15:12 where he said, "This is my commandment, That ye love one another, as I have loved you." John takes them back to the Gospel. He is not trying to give them a watered-down version of the Gospel or the Gospel with a twist on it. He gives them the old commandment from the beginning. John says the old will still do.

In this modern age of liberalism and false teachers, we need to cling to the old Book. Preaching and teaching are not about uncovering something new; it's about explaining and revealing something that is old. This is what makes the Word of God so special. Our God never changes, and so it stands to reason that His Word never changes. We must believe the Bible for what it is and what it says. As it has been said by many, "We do not need to rewrite it; we just need to reread it."

If you are a Bible reader and a Bible believer, then you understand the importance of staying with the Word of God. Nothing new will do. Just give me the old commandments from the Book. John says in this verse that it was right in the beginning, and it is still relevant now. There is assurance in the consistency of its message. Thank the Lord that we have a Bible that still reads the same. Others can say what they will and do as they please, but I will take the old Book!

"An Old Book with a New Message"

1 John 2:8 – *"Again, a new commandment I write unto you, which thing is true in him and in you: because the darkness is past, and the true light now shineth."*

Reading the Bible can sometimes be a mystery. John announces in verse seven that he is not writing a new commandment, but an old commandment from the beginning. Now, in verse eight, he announces he is writing a new commandment. This seems to be contradictory. However, when you read John's message, it lines up perfectly with the message of Jesus. The Gospel of John and the Epistle of John coincide.

John reveals both the light and the life that is within the message. The Bible is the only book that is old, yet its message is always new. It is new to the sinner who has never heard it. The Bible is new to the sinner who has often heard it but has for the first time believed it. The Bible is new to the believer every time he opens it and reads it. Every day, this old Book has a new message for our lives. The Bible is new for current and future events. It's older than any book on the shelf, but it is more up-to-date than the newspaper that will run tomorrow.

This is how John could say in one verse that he is writing an old commandment, and then in the next verse say he is writing a new commandment. Our Bible is an old book with a new message. The life and light of this book are what make it new every time it is read or spoken. This should encourage us to stay in the Book because it gives light to all avenues of life. Though the message is old, it can still be new to you today if you will read and study it. Take the time to share it with someone who has never heard or received this message.

"Living in the Darkness of Hatred"

1 John 2:9 – *"He that saith he is in the light, and hateth his brother, is in darkness even until now."*

Hatred is a very evil sin. The seeds of hatred may go undetected in the beginning; however, over time, they can grow inwardly like cancer. If this evil seed is cultivated in one's heart, it can destroy both the individual and those around him. Hatred will produce other sinful seeds, such as stubbornness, pride, anger, murder, and malice. These are only a few, to say the least.

Remember, that hatred doesn't have to have a cause. Hatred is the cause. Hatred will blind an individual. It will cause you to be blind to the truth, blind to the consequences of your actions, and blind to the effects it has on yourself and those whom you love. Hatred can even cause a soul to go to hell. A good example of this would be one of the thieves on the cross. He died blind to his need, blind to his Savior, and blind to his opportunity to be saved.

There are many today who are walking in the darkness of hatred. Life is too short, and eternity is too long to live one second in this darkness. You must step out of the darkness of hatred and into the light of God's love. Ask the Lord for mercy and to help you be merciful. Ask Him to give you grace and to help you to be gracious. Ask for His forgiveness, and ask Him to help you show forgiveness.

Our verse makes it clear that a person cannot be walking in the light of God's love and living in the darkness of hatred. Yet, some claim to be in fellowship with God and refuse to fellowship with their brothers in Christ. While they may fool themselves, they are not fooling others. Allow God's Word to rid you of any seeds of hatred that may try to grow in your soul. Live each day in the sunlight of His love.

"Helping Others Along the Way"

1 John 2:10 – *"He that loveth his brother abideth in the light, and there is none occasion of stumbling in him."*

Brotherly love is so vital within the church. The devil knows if he can cause division or strife in any assembly, he can weaken their spiritual power. This will cause the people to lose focus and get off track. If they do manage to carry on, things will become mechanical, and their passion for things of God will be drastically altered. They will become a church of performance rather than a church of power.

John teaches in this verse that brotherly love is an act of obedience. When we display brotherly love, we are abiding in the light of God's Word. We are to love the brethren because it is biblical. We do not get to pick and choose, nor do we hold a grudge when we feel a brother is not displaying love back.

Another reason we are to show brotherly love is that it strengthens the brethren. Brotherly love is a great example and expression of God's love. This helps other brothers along the way. The Bible says in 1 Corinthians 13:8, "Charity never faileth." Just as it's never right to show hate, it is always right to show love.

Love never compromises, love never criticizes, and love never categorizes. Love is balanced, love is bold, love is beautiful, and love is beneficial. Love helps those who are discouraged, those who are defeated, and those who are despised. I challenge all of us to strive now more than ever to show Christian love. Today, let's help others along the way with acts of love. Find some brother who needs to be loved, and reach out to him. Go the extra mile by helping him or fellowshipping with him. Ask God to put a brother in your path that is about to stumble, and allow the love of God to work through you toward them.

"Blinded Eyes"

1 John 2:11 – *"But he that hateth his brother is in darkness, and walketh in darkness, and knoweth not whither he goeth, because that darkness hath blinded his eyes."*

It is possible for a man to have eyes that can physically see and still live a blinded life. What is even more surprising is for a man to have his spiritual eyes open and live a blinded life. You might ask yourself, how could this happen? How can a man see physically and spiritually, yet live as though he could not see at all?

The answer is rather simple. The man in our verse is blind, not because he cannot see, but because he chooses not to see. He has chosen to walk the dark alley of hatred. He knows it's a dark trail, and he knows there is no light along the way, but he chooses to walk its path in spite of the darkness.

Just because you and I have physical eyes that can see, it does not mean we can walk the dark alleys of this world without any light. We must have light on our path. We cannot put blinders on our eyes and expect to see through them. As foolish as this sounds, some have chosen to be blinded by hatred toward another. Friend, no matter how saved you are, or how spiritual you think you may be, hatred will blind your eyes. It will cause you to lose your way in this world because you are leaving the light of God's Word whenever you hate. As our verse says, "knoweth not whither he goeth."

Those who profess to know Christ but have no genuine love for the brethren are living a false profession. When sinners get saved, they step out of the darkness into the light. They become a part of the family of God and demonstrate genuine love toward their brothers and sisters in Christ.

"Your Sins Are Forgiven"

1 John 2:12 – *"I write unto you, little children, because your sins are forgiven you for his name's sake."*

John directs this verse to those who are young in the faith. He wants them to understand why he has written this Epistle. They need to be reminded of what God has done in their lives. Also, he wants them to understand why the Lord has shown this great act of kindness.

They were once sinners guilty before God. They were unable to save themselves and incapable of paying the enormous sin debt that belonged to them. The debt was greater than they could ever imagine. All they could do is plead guilty as charged before Him. They were a slave to sin and Satan. For what looked hopeless to those who were helpless, God in mercy forgave them. He wiped their slate clean and stamped the charges paid in full. Their sins have been forgiven!

What joy to have your sins forgiven! This is true for all who accept His mercy and trust the finished work of Calvary. The problem is, often a believer loses sight of this forgiveness. If we are not careful, we can become numb to the privilege that God has extended to us. Asking for forgiveness of our sins is something that we should be practicing daily in our lives. As we approach God in prayer and ask for daily cleansing and forgiveness, we should thank Him for this privilege. We should never fail to take advantage of this opportunity in our lives. The forgiveness of sins is a faithful promise we can always rely on.

We must be reminded as to why. Why would God show such loving kindness? Why would He go to such great lengths to forgive us? The answer is in our verse. The Bible says, "for his name's sake." We are forgiven because of Jesus. Jesus paid it all, and all to Him we owe.

"We Have It in Writing"

1 John 2:13 – *"I write unto you, fathers, because ye have known him that is from the beginning. I write unto you, young men, because ye have overcome the wicked* one. I write unto you, little children, because ye have known the Father."

John uses the phrase "I write unto you" three times in this verse. We should take careful note of the significant meaning of this phrase. It will tell us who John is writing to, what he is writing about, and why he is writing these things.

First, he writes to the fathers. These are the more mature, wiser saints. He is addressing believers who have faithfully walked with the Master for many years. Their lives testify to their deeper walk with God. They are pillars of faith, examples to follow, and honorable Christians who have blazed a trail for others to follow.

Secondly, he addresses the young men. These are the ones who may not have the years behind them, but they have stood tall in the battle for God. They are strong in their faith and have not wavered in their convictions. When we think of a young man, we think of his ability, his strength, and his energy. What he lacks in wisdom, he makes up for in zeal. He has won some victories in his Christian life and defeated Satan.

Finally, he addresses the children. Those who are young in faith but have the help and encouragement of the older and stronger saints. We will say more about this matter in our next devotional. What a blessing to know that John wrote these addresses down because they still exist today. Every congregation should be made up of these same three classifications of believers. We have in writing where we are to start in our faith and where we are to end. The question is, where do I see myself today?

"Helping the Young"

1 John 2:14 – *"I have written unto you, fathers, because ye have known him that is from the beginning. I have written unto you, young men, because ye are strong, and the word of God abideth in you, and ye have overcome the wicked one."*

John again reminds the fathers and young men why he has written to them. The fathers are the spiritual leaders of the church, and the young men are the strong warriors of the church. The young have received a personal admonishment from him in verse twelve, but here John has a different purpose in mind. He does not address the young but has a message to other believers that will help them.

John knew the value of helping those who were young in their faith. He also knew the blessing of one believer aiding another. There are several areas from which we draw our spiritual strength. The Scriptures, the Spirit, the sanctuary, and service are only a few of those areas. The saints of God are another area from which we draw strength. We have the ability to serve others, and it is a blessing to do so.

Remember, we all need help, and we can all help one another, especially those who are young in the faith. If you are a young Christian, recognize that God has surrounded you with saints who can help you. If you have been a Christian for a while, then remember that it was not that long ago that you sat where they are. Help strengthen the young. If you are an aged Christian, do not get frustrated with the lack of maturity seen in those who are young. Your ministry is to be patient with them and help them along the road of life. Finally, we must all remember those who have helped us and those who are helping us. Pray for God to put wise and strong saints in your path as you go through life. While ministering, guard against pride and the arrogance of thinking that you are something special. Humility alone will greatly help the young.

"Worldly Passions"

1 John 2:15 – *"Love not the world, neither the things that are in the world. If any man love the world, the love of the Father is not in him."*

The word used for "world" is *kosmos*. This word has a considerable amount of meaning. It can be used to represent creation, humanity, and a system. For example, when the Bible speaks of the Lord making this world, it is speaking about its Creation. When it tells us that God loves the world, it is speaking of the world's humanity. When the Bible commands us not to love the world, it is speaking of its system. It is teaching us to avoid worldly passions.

One reason to avoid worldly passions is that one worldly passion leads to another. Our verse says, "Love not the world, NEITHER the THINGS that are in the world." Did you notice how loving the world's system can lead to loving the world's content? Worldly passions will always grow beyond our expectations, pulling us further in every day. We have all said, "I'm just going to do this one thing," or "I'm not going to go as far as they did with it." We are so foolish to think we can handle the world's system and its substance.

Another reason to avoid worldly passions is that it robs us of our relationship with our Father. Just like an unfaithful husband who loses his love and appreciation for his wife, a believer who is in a relationship with the world will lose his love for his Father. The prodigal in Luke 15 lost his love for his father when he got his eyes on worldly goods and pleasures. It was not until he lost everything that he came home broken and humiliated. At that moment, he found true love in his father's arms. When he had nothing to show for his foolish choices, the father loved him. Friend, the world does not love you, and the world will not profit you. Do not be fooled by worldly passions. Love not the world!

"Worldly Pleasures"

1 John 2:16 – *"For all that is in the world, the lust of the flesh, and the lust of the eyes, and the pride of life, is not of the Father, but is of the world."*

This world has many sinful pleasures. The Bible teaches us that those pleasures are only for a season. These worldly pleasures are not worth the price we will have to pay to enjoy them. To avoid these worldly pleasures, we must be aware of what they are. The problem is that there are so many pleasures in this world; where do we begin?

Our verse today sums up worldly pleasures in three basic categories: the lust of the flesh, which has to do with appetites; the lust of the eyes, which has to do with appearance; and the pride of life, which has to do with applause. All the sinful pleasures of this world can be found in one of these three categories.

It has often been said that an individual will fight the lust of the flesh in their youth, they will battle the lust of the eye in their middle age, and they will face the pride of life in their golden years. This does not mean that we won't have issues with these worldly pleasures at any point in our lives. A teenager can battle the pride of life, and an elderly man can battle the lust of the flesh. But it does mean that these specific pleasures are most common with these specific age brackets.

Worldly pleasures do not come from the Father. The Bible is clear to point this out in this verse. They are of the world. We live in a day when people want to attach the Lord's name to a lot of worldly pleasures. God has never put His stamp of approval on the sinful pleasures of this world, and neither should we. Do not let the pleasures of this world have control of your life today.

"Worldly Passings"

1 John 2:17 – *"And the world passeth away, and the lust thereof: but he that doeth the will of God abideth for ever."*

This verse contains a world that is passing and a will that is profitable. If we, as believers, pursue the will of God over the things of this world, then we have an assurance that it will profit us in this world and in the world to come. God's will is permanent, and the world is passing.

Time is forever passing in this world. Man cannot stop time, nor can he make more time. Each of us has an allotted time given by God to live in this world. If we are slothful and lazy, time will pass us by. Time waits for no man, for it has a destination also. One day, time will be no more.

Treasures are forever passing. Things are handed down from one generation to another. With the most careful preservation and security, they are eaten away by moths and rust. Sometimes they are stolen by thieves, just as Jesus predicted. The treasures of this world will not last forever because they are not meant to last forever. They are passing away in the rust and the dust of this world.

Titles are forever passing. No position of authority or royalty in this world is forever. Kings and queens, presidents, and prime ministers who serve today are only filling the shoes of others who walked before them. They will one day lay down their position of honor to another because titles are not forever. They are passing with the world every day.

Though the world passes away, the things of God are eternal! His Word, His will, and His work will stand forever and ever. One day, we will live in a world that will never pass away. We will live with Christ our King!

"Time Is Running Out!"

1 John 2:18 – *"Little children, it is the last time: and as ye have heard that antichrist shall come, even now are there many antichrists; whereby we know that it is the last time."*

John wants the "little children" to be aware of both the time in which they are living and the dangers of the time in which they are living. This is good for all believers, but the strong and mature should already be aware of these facts. Our text shows us the value of discipleship in the lives of young Christians. We must make them aware of what we are facing, so they can grow and withstand the false teachings around them.

John gives them both a past warning and a present warning in this verse. He reminds them that they have heard that the antichrist will come. He also reminds them that there are many antichrists, or false teachers, surrounding them at that moment. Twice, he emphasized that "it is the last time." New Testament believers were looking for Jesus to come in their lifetimes. They were quick to mark all of those who were "antichrist." They were not "the Antichrist," but they were those who taught against Christ and His teachings.

If John was warning young believers in his day, how much more should we be warning believers in our day? If the early church believers were aware that it was the last time, how much more should we be mindful of this truth? The difference is that they were looking for Christ to come, whereas today, many believers are not. The truth of this text is that time is quickly running out. Everything that was true in this verse at that time is one thousand times truer today! Time was running out in John's day. False teachers and doctrines were warring against believers in the New Testament times. Think about this verse now. All of this proves that the sand in the hourglass of time is about gone. Time is running out!

"Spiritual Betrayal"

1 John 2:19 – *"They went out from us, but they were not of us; for if they had been of us, they would no doubt have continued with us: but they went out, that they might be made manifest that they were not all of us."*

The church is encouraged when people are added to the membership. It always boosts the morale and strengthens the congregation to see new faces sitting in the pews. The absence of membership has the reverse effect on the church. It can be disheartening to see people leave and go to another church or get out altogether.

The people in our verse are not simply backsliders but apostates who have left the church due to false teaching. False doctrine has led them away and has revealed who they really are. I understand that anyone can be led astray. However, there are some who join our ranks, sing our songs, and learn our lingo, but miss out on the reality of Christianity. Truth is what holds everything together, and whenever someone lacks truth, they will eventually abandon those who hold to it.

We must remember that when someone leaves the church, they are not walking away from us, they are walking away from Christ. They are walking away from the light of God's Word. John teaches us in this verse that spiritual betrayal affects the individual's fellowship with the church and reveals the absence of their faith in Christ. Many faces came to my mind when I read this verse. I asked myself, "Are these individuals truly saved?" Only God knows the answer to that question. It makes me appreciate both my fellowship with the church and my relationship with Christ. By God's grace, determine to stay in the church you are serving in, and always keep your relationship with the Savior right.

"Spiritual Guidance"

1 John 2:20 – *"But ye have an unction from the Holy One, and ye know all things."*

The word "unction" is translated from the Greek word "chrisma," which means "the anointed One". The word Christ stems from this same word. Though the Person of Christ is not with us, He was with the apostles, but His Spirit is with us today. The presence of Jesus lives in our hearts through the indwelling of the Holy Spirit. Every true believer is indwelled with the Holy Spirit at the moment of salvation.

Once the Holy Spirit moves into our hearts, He immediately begins to work in our lives. He gives the new believer understanding of the Scriptures and speaks to him in a personal manner. The Spirit of God never guides us against the Word of God. They are always in perfect harmony with each other.

The Spirit's guidance is important when it comes to false doctrine. Many have tried to overcome false doctrine by studying the occults. There is no need for us to spend hours studying heresy. We should not waste our time trying to learn all we can about the apostates of our day. We are instructed to know the truth. The more we read and understand the Bible, the more we will be able to identify the heresy. The Holy Spirit will turn the light on in our hearts when we are faced with anything that is not sound.

As believers, we should be inspired to grow for the Lord. We should yield to the "Holy One" in our lives and allow the fullness of His Spirit to control us. Being filled with the Scriptures and with the Spirit will give us all of the knowledge and wisdom that we will need to serve God effectively. Daily prayer and Bible study are essential for every child of God. It not only strengthens us inwardly, but it guides us outwardly into the right way. Make Bible reading, prayer, and yielding to the Spirit a part of your everyday routine.

"This Is Worth Repeating"

1 John 2:21 – *"I have not written unto you because ye know not the truth, but because ye know it, and that no lie is of the truth."*

I remember a Bible college teacher who often used a particular quote when he wanted to challenge us to study. He would say, "A good Bible student is a student of the Bible to his grave." This has stayed with me down through the years and has served as a reminder of the importance of learning and relearning what has been written.

I'm sure you have heard the saying, "anything worth saying once is worth repeating twice." John certainly believed this and states it in our verse. He is not writing something new to these believers, but he is simply reinforcing what has already been said. Repetition is important because it helps to reinforce the truth that we have been given.

True believers who have a love for the truth do not mind repetition. While we are learning new truths in the Word of God, it is still good to be reminded of what we have heard and already know. The Gospel has been preached over and over in the presence of the saints, but how pleasant it is each time we hear it. The old story never grows old because it is true.

Truth is what makes something worth repeating. Our verse is clear that truth and lies are mutually exclusive. We can repeat the Bible again and again because it is all truth and free from all lies. Those who doubt the truths of the Bible will believe a lie. For there is nothing else to believe if you reject the truth. Those who receive the truth will forever love it and want to hear it time and time again. If you know the truth, then you know you don't need anything else. You don't need something new and improved because you are satisfied by hearing what has helped you down through the years. I close with a quote from an old song that says, "Oh, tell me that story, that story so precious." Truth doesn't have to be new; it just needs to be repeated.

"The World's Biggest Liar"

1 John 2:22 – *"Who is a liar but he that denieth that Jesus is the Christ? He is antichrist, that denieth the Father and the Son."*

I recently read an article on the study of lying. Psychologists say the average person lies two to three times every ten minutes. While reading the article, I must confess, I wondered if it was true or a lie. It certainly sounds unbelievable.

There are three things that never cease to amaze me about lying: those who tell the lie, the content of the lie, and those who choose to believe the lie. Some are very clever when it comes to telling a lie, and others are transparent from the start. This reminds me of a lady who was renting in an apartment complex. The landlord had a strict rule that tenants could have cats living in their apartment, but no dogs. Whenever the renter was reported for her dog barking, she replied to her landlord that "she would never have a dog, this was a special breed of cat, that was called a dog-cat."

There is no other way for me to say it, but the woman in the story told a big lie. A lie that was so far from the truth that it seemed beyond reason. Even though that was a big lie, it's not the biggest lie ever told. The biggest lie ever told is found in our text. To say that Jesus is not the Christ is the world's biggest lie. This is a lie that the world has been trying to convince each other of since Christ came into this world. Those who proclaim this lie are called liars here in the Word of God.

The way to defeat these antichrists is by spreading the truth of the Gospel. A lie may sprint ahead of the truth to start with, but be patient, truth always prevails in the end. One day the embodiment of Truth, Jesus, will cast the father of lies, Satan, into the lake of fire. Heaven will be all about Jesus, and we will live every day in truth. We will live in a land where there are no lies or deceptions.

"Father and Son"

1 John 2:23 – "Whosoever denieth the Son, the same hath not the Father: (but) he that acknowledgeth the Son hath the Father also."

You cannot have one without the other. The only way to have a right relationship with God is to have a real relationship with Christ. Many in this world claim to know God but reject Christ. They want nothing to do with Christianity, nothing to do with the cross, and nothing to do with those who believe.

Our verse is very simple. If you deny Jesus, then you know not God. If you accept Jesus, then you have God as your Heavenly Father. What a tragedy for many, and what a triumph for those who acknowledge the Son. We know that Jesus is God, for the Bible says in Colossians 1:19, "For it pleased the Father that in Him should all fullness dwell." The Father dwells in the Son and the Son in the Father, see John 14:10-11. This makes them inseparable.

Those who would teach that you can have the Father without the Son, are not only wrong but John wants us to see they are antichrists. This is as offensive to God as it would be to any earthly father. There is not a father who loves his son, that would allow someone to accept him, but not his son.

God did what no earthly father could do or would do. He gave His only begotten Son that man could be saved. The Son loved the Father and humanity so much that He was willing to give His life. If a man wants to bypass the Son of God, he will never enter into heaven's portals. The Son dwells with the Father and will be with Him in eternity. Have you accepted the Son? Will you be with the Father in eternity?

"An Abiding Friend"

1 John 2:24 – *"Let that therefore abide in you, which ye have heard from the beginning. If that which ye have heard from the beginning shall remain in you, ye also shall continue in the Son, and in the Father."*

Salvation not only delivers our soul from hell but gives us a friend that is like no other. Proverbs 18:24 says, "A man that hath friends must shew himself friendly: and there is a friend that sticketh closer than a brother." We know that friend is Jesus! He abides with us just as He said He would in John chapter fifteen.

How is this possible? Scripture teaches us that while Jesus is at the right hand of the Father, He has not left us alone. He has given us His Spirit in our hearts to abide with us. This means from the moment of salvation, the Spirit moves in and works in our lives. He is there constantly to help us whenever and wherever He is needed. He will guide us, comfort us, convict us and instruct us if we will be sensitive to Him.

The Holy Spirit will never lead us astray from the Father, nor the Son. Just as they are in perfect harmony, a believer who is yielded to the Spirit will be in harmony. What a blessing to know that His Spirit lives within us! What assurance to know He will continue to abide with us!

Christ made every provision necessary for us before He left this world. He did not leave us comfortless. He commands that we abide in Him. We can abide in Him through daily prayer and daily Bible reading. These are essentials for maintaining a healthy and happy relationship with the Father and the Son. Allow His Spirit to control your life. Do not struggle through life by trying to serve God in your own power and strength. Abide in Christ and find the rest you need.

"A Promise That Is Out of This World"

1 John 2:25 – *"And this is the promise that he hath promised us, even eternal life."*

A promise can be no greater than the one who is making the promise. Some people make promises that they cannot keep. Others make promises that they can keep, but their track record of keeping promises is not very good. Promise-keeping is not always an easy task.

Here we have a promise that is out of this world. This promise goes beyond the realm of time. It goes beyond the realm of physical life. It goes beyond the realm of humanity. There is not a man on earth that could make this promise and keep it. This is the greatest promise that has ever been made. I want to explain why this is so.

First, it is the greatest promise ever made because of the One who made the promise. Our Creator made us this promise. God the Father has promised every believer eternal life. He is the ultimate promise keeper because the Lord has kept every promise He has ever made.

Another reason is because of the promise itself. God is the giver of life. We have all been blessed to have been given physical life. God is promising us something even greater than physical life. He has promised eternal life.

Finally, this is the greatest promise because of the price it cost to give us such a gift. Salvation may be free, but it's certainly not cheap. Jesus paid it all on Calvary, so we could have eternal life. It cost the Father His only Son. It cost the Son His life. It costs us nothing. All we must do is receive the gift of life. Oh, what a price! Oh, what a pardon! Oh, what a promise!

"A Spiritual Word in a Seducing World"

1 John 2:26 – *"These things have I written unto you concerning them that seduce you."*

The word "seduce" means to draw away from what is right. This is how Satan works against man. He makes false doctrine appealing to the flesh to lure men away from the truth. He organizes religion, makes it attractive, and fills his teaching with seducers who are full of charisma and charm, to catch the attention of those with whom they come in contact. His ultimate goal is to get men to believe anything other than the truth.

John is concerned about believers being seduced by false teachers, so he writes this Epistle to them. Let us be reminded that the Epistle he is writing is the Word of God. We do not need to study false doctrine to overcome its teaching; all we need is the truth. The Bible is the answer for defeating any Satanic seduction we might encounter.

We live in a time when believers are easily drawn away. Failure to read and study God's Word is the result of this sad commentary. Attending a Bible-believing and preaching church will help, but it is not enough. Faithful attendance to Sunday School is a must for every believer, but it is not enough. Even a Godly heritage and family altar are commendable, but they are still not a substitute for our own personal devotion. To keep from being drawn away by these seducers, we must daily feed on the Word of God.

We must not be deceived into thinking that we are above being seduced. This would be the first sign of letting down your guard. Greater Christians than any of us have been swept away by false teaching and doctrine. The only thing that a seducer needs is a listening ear. Make up your mind to be a student of the Bible all the days of your life.

"The Ministry of the Holy Spirit"

1 John 2:27 – *"But the anointing which ye have received of him abideth in you, and ye need not that any man teach you: but as the same anointing teacheth you of all things, and is truth, and is no lie, and even as it hath taught you, ye shall abide in him."*

The ministry of the Holy Spirit is clearly seen in the Word of God. John 16:7-11 teaches us that He has a ministry of reproving the world. In John 3:1-8, He has a ministry of regenerating the lost. The Holy Spirit also has a ministry of restraining the wicked, in 2 Thess. 2:3-8.

The Spirit's work in the life of a believer is just as evident through other New Testament verses. In 1 Cor. 12:13, He baptizes the believer into the body of Christ. In Romans 8:8, He gives the believer gifts. And, according to Eph. 1:13, He seals the believer at the moment of salvation. Once He indwells the believer, He then actively fills the believer as he surrenders to His leadership.

Our verse gives us five amazing truths about the Holy Spirit's ministry. First, we see that He abides in us. Second, He is always the same. Third, He teaches us all things. Fourth, He only teaches us what is true. And finally, He will never teach us a lie. Time would not allow us to comment on these wonderful blessings, but it should encourage us to walk in the Spirit daily.

Too often, we are guilty of ignoring His ministry and leadership in our lives. We try to handle things ourselves when we don't have to. We should look to the Spirit for guidance and allow His ministry to be fulfilled within us. Our ministry should be allowing His ministry to take hold of us every day. Allow the Spirit to control and lead you in the direction God wants for your life.

"Rapture Ready"

1 John 2:28 – *"And now, little children, abide in him; that, when he shall appear, we may have confidence, and not be ashamed before him at his coming."*

I remember, as a young teenage boy, hearing preachers constantly preaching on the rapture. They were warning sinners to get right because Jesus may come at any moment. They would remind them that if the rapture took place, and they were not ready, they would be left behind to face God's wrath and judgment.

They would encourage the saints to stay busy and fervent, so they would not be ashamed when He comes. We don't hear as much of that preaching as we used to, but it's still in the Book. Our text is not speaking to the lost but to the saved. John is telling the saints that they need to be ready for the rapture at any moment. To be saved, but not rapture-ready, means you will be ashamed when He comes. This is what our verse states. However, we do not have to be ashamed. If we will follow the Spirit's leadership in our lives, and surrender to Him, we can have confidence when He comes. We can be looking for and anticipating His coming.

The church used to be filled with saints who were ready for the rapture. They would come to church ready to worship and go home ready to witness. Most churches today have lost sight of this great truth. They have lost hope or have become so worldly that they do not want Him to come. They like the world they live in too much for it to be interrupted with His coming. They do not long for His return as they once did. Despite the apathy we see today, I have good news: Jesus is still coming again! The rapture is at hand! Live your life today in light of the truth that He could come at any moment. Make every decision today based on this one truth, and you will find yourself rapture-ready!

"A Righteous Birth"

1 John 2:29 – "If ye know that he is righteous, ye know that every one that doeth righteousness is born of him."

A righteous birth will produce a righteous life. This is a fundamental truth that cannot be ignored. There is another fundamental truth: you and I are not righteous. We can never be righteous within ourselves, and we can never obtain righteousness by ourselves. These thoughts will help us to place this verse in context.

First, we see who is righteous. John says we know that He is Righteous. There is no argument when it comes to the righteousness of Christ. He is the perfect Lamb of God. Pilate stated he found no fault in Jesus, and it has been echoed by all who have investigated Him. Nothing can be laid to His charge. He had a righteous birth, lived a righteous life, and died a righteous death. The world testified at His death that He truly was the Son of God.

Those who have received Christ as their Savior have received His righteousness. His righteousness has been placed upon them. I'm glad I can say I have traded my filthy rags for His robe of righteousness. When God sees me, He does not see my garments of sin; He sees His Son. He sees me as worthy when He looks through the blood of Calvary's cross. I'm so glad the blood covers all of our sins.

As saints, we are not perfect, but we are forgiven. We can find daily cleansing and renewal. Our position never changes because it is anchored in His righteousness. We should get up every day and thank the Lord for the salvation He has provided and the security He has given in the righteousness of Jesus Christ. Do not be fooled by the filthy garments of religion. It may dress you up, but Christ will clean you up. He will give you a righteous birth that will produce a righteous life.

1 John 3

1 Behold, what manner of love the Father hath bestowed upon us, that we should be called the sons of God: therefore the world knoweth us not, because it knew him not.

2 Beloved, now are we the sons of God, and it doth not yet appear what we shall be: but we know that, when he shall appear, we shall be like him; for we shall see him as he is.

3 And every man that hath this hope in him purifieth himself, even as he is pure.

4 Whosoever committeth sin transgresseth also the law: for sin is the transgression of the law.

5 And ye know that he was manifested to take away our sins; and in him is no sin.

6 Whosoever abideth in him sinneth not: whosoever sinneth hath not seen him, neither known him.

7 Little children, let no man deceive you: he that doeth righteousness is righteous, even as he is righteous.

8 He that committeth sin is of the devil; for the devil sinneth from the beginning. For this purpose the Son of God was manifested, that he might destroy the works of the devil.

9 Whosoever is born of God doth not commit sin; for his seed remaineth in him: and he cannot sin, because he is born of God.

10 In this the children of God are manifest, and the children of the devil: whosoever doeth not righteousness is not of God, neither he that loveth not his brother.

11 For this is the message that ye heard from the beginning, that we should love one another.

12 Not as Cain, who was of that wicked one, and slew his brother. And wherefore slew he him? Because his own works were evil, and his brother's righteous.

13 Marvel not, my brethren, if the world hate you.

14 We know that we have passed from death unto life, because we love the brethren. He that loveth not his brother abideth in death.

15 Whosoever hateth his brother is a murderer: and ye know that no murderer hath eternal life abiding in him.

16 Hereby perceive we the love of God, because he laid down his life for us: and we ought to lay down our lives for the brethren.

17 But whoso hath this world's good, and seeth his brother have need, and shutteth up his bowels of compassion from him, how dwelleth the love of God in him?

18 My little children, let us not love in word, neither in tongue; but in deed and in truth.

19 And hereby we know that we are of the truth, and shall assure our hearts before him.

20 For if our heart condemn us, God is greater than our heart, and knoweth all things.

21 Beloved, if our heart condemn us not, then have we confidence toward God.

22 And whatsoever we ask, we receive of him, because we keep his commandments, and do those things that are pleasing in his sight.

23 And this is his commandment, That we should believe on the name of his Son Jesus Christ, and love one another, as he gave us commandment.

24 And he that keepeth his commandments dwelleth in him, and he in him. And hereby we know that he abideth in us, by the Spirit which he hath given us.

"What Love Divine!"

1 John 3:1 – "Behold, what manner of love the Father hath bestowed upon us, that we should be called the sons of God: therefore the world knoweth us not, because it knew him not."

Several years ago, I heard the story of a man who was standing at the top of a tall building in New York City. He was preparing to jump off the top of the building and commit suicide. Some of the people of the city had gathered around the skyscraper and began to chant for the man to jump. He could hear them as their voices were lifted, "Jump! jump! jump!"

Someone cried out to the man and asked, "Why are you jumping?" He replied, "Because no one loves me. My parents gave me away when I was a child, and I have lived in foster care all of my life. My foster parents abused me and didn't want me around. Recently, my fiancé ran off with another man, and I am left alone." He said, "All of my life, all I've ever wanted is for someone to love me. I'm 24 years old, and no one cares. Now I'm going to end my life."

About that time, a police officer approached the edge of the building where the man was. He said to him, "Son, I'll love you if you will just come down from this building. If you will take me by the hand, my wife and I will adopt you. We were never able to have children, and I have wanted a son like you all of my life." The man took the police officer by the hand, and at 24 years of age, he was adopted by the officer and his wife.

I remember when I was standing out on the edge of life. The demons of hell were crying, jump! Jesus stretched forth His hand and rescued me. What manner of love has been bestowed upon us as the children of God! We have been loved, adopted, rescued, and brought into the family of God. This is love that the world has never experienced. It is divine love!

"A Cinderella Story!"

1 John 3:2 – *"Beloved, now are we the sons of God, and it doth not yet appear what we shall be: but we know that, when he shall appear, we shall be like him; for we shall see him as he is."*

Most of us can remember from our childhood days the fairytale "Cinderella." We recall the evil stepmother and her two daughters who mistreated the damsel and saw her only as a slave to their household. Cinderella was poor, unwanted, and unloved by those whom she served daily. Her life seemed hopeless until one day a fairy godmother granted her a wish that brought her to the palace of a prince. The prince instantly fell in love with her. He sought after Cinderella and rescued her. He then took her to the palace, where she became his wife, and they lived happily ever after.

This story is a beautiful piece of literature that has been read and enjoyed by many. The only problem is that none of it is true. It is just a fairytale. However, our text gives us a true Cinderella story. It reminds us of how we were just like the character in the story, a slave to this world, unwanted and unloved. We were mistreated by the devil, with no hope in sight. Then the Lord came along and sought us through tender compassion and love. He rescued us from the prison of sin we were in and brought us into the family of God.

Our story may not seem like much of a Cinderella story at the present, but it could change at any moment. The Prince of Peace will one day come riding in, and we are going to be changed from rags to riches. We will be swept away by His love and carried to His palace. His bride will then be complete, and we will enjoy the pleasures in His palace and live happily ever after. Our Cinderella story is true and will happen when He shall appear!

"Keeping Us on Our Toes"

1 John 3:3 – *"And every man that hath this hope in him purifieth himself, even as he is pure."*

The phrase "keeping me on my toes" is one that we are all familiar with. It means the individual is being helped to stay on top of things. They are being held accountable while being encouraged to strive for their best performance. We have all experienced this in life. We have all had someone, or something, "keep us on our toes."

When we think about the rapture and the events that are to follow, this phrase comes to mind. John says this hope helps us to purify our lives. In other words, it helps to "keep the believer on his toes." It causes us to press forward and to examine our lives because the rapture could take place at any moment. The hope of Christ's return should bring about the best performance in our daily lives. This hope is the fundamental truth that should hold us accountable in our service and our personal walk with Him.

Having said that, why are so many Christians not living in this manner? The answer is simple: they have lost sight of this hope. If we are not careful, we can become so consumed with living down here that we forget that He could come at any moment. We have stopped looking for His return. This will cause apathy and complacency to take control of our lives. These are deadly characteristics that will weaken our performance and can even lead to an unholy lifestyle.

We must purify our lives through the Word of God and prayer. We must constantly be moving forward, or we will backslide. The greatest motivator is the truth that He is coming, and it just might be today. This hope should "keep us on our toes" in our Christian lives. Allow this hope to purify your walk with Him today.

"Fact or Fiction"

1 John 3:4 – *"Whosoever committeth sin transgresseth also the law: for sin is the transgression of the law."*

If you believe the Bible, then you believe it to be a book of facts and not fiction. So, what about this verse? Read it carefully and think about it. If we are now under grace, and not the law, then how is it that we transgress the law? Many teach that because we are living under grace, the law is not effective in the lives of New Testament believers. They say that we can throw away the rule book, live as we please, and do as we will because we are no longer under the law, but under grace. Amid all of this confusion, I simply want to point out what is fact and what is fiction. Our text verse will help us to do this.

It is a fact that we are not under the law anymore as a system. We are now living in the dispensation of grace. Grace is a much better system to live under than the old economy. We are saved by grace through faith in the Lord Jesus Christ. Again, all of this is a Bible fact.

Though the law may not be our system in this dispensation, it is still our standard. The law defines what sin is and how seriously God takes sin. The law reveals that the world is under condemnation and that all men are sinners. The law proves that our standard could never measure up to God's standard. The law reveals our need for a Savior.

The fact is, sin is the transgression of the law. Even though the law is not the system we are living by, it should still be the standard by which we view sin. The law allows us to see sin as God sees it. The law helps us to measure sin by His standard and not our own. This will produce holy living, rather than reckless living. It will also separate what is fact and what is fiction.

"The Sinless Savior"

1 John 3:5 – *"And ye know that he was manifested to take away our sins; and in him is no sin."*

This verse contains two wonderful truths about our Savior. The first truth is that He came to take away our sins. The second truth is that He is sinless. Had Jesus not been sinless, He could have never taken our sins away. John says we know both of these to be a fact because His life was manifested before us. Jesus lived a sinless life for all the world to see. Though the Pharisees and others tried to destroy Him and find fault, they failed. Pilate himself declared, "I find no fault in Him".

The Gospels also declared His sinless life and His death on the cross. They tell how He was buried, and three days later He arose victorious over death, hell, and the grave. He could not have done this had He not been the perfect sacrifice. He is the only begotten Son of God! He is the Lamb of God! He is our Redeemer and Lord!

What peace we find in this sinless Savior! He took all of our sins away. As the songwriter stated, "My sins not in part, but the whole, have been nailed to the cross, and I bear them no more." This includes our past, present, and future sins. We are no longer under the bondage of sin. We have been set free through Jesus Christ.

Make it your goal today to tell someone about Christ. Many are slaves to sin, and we have the answer to their freedom. Share the Gospel message of Christ with someone you come in contact with today. Tell them about a sinless Savior who died to rescue them from the bondage of sin. Tell them of His love and mercy that has been extended to their soul. Tell them how He is willing to save them if they will trust Him with all their heart.

"The Difference Between the Two"

1 John 3:6 – *"Whosoever abideth in him sinneth not: whosoever sinneth hath not seen him, neither known him."*

We should carefully consider this verse. John is not saying that when someone gets saved they reach sinless perfection. He is not teaching that once you put your faith in Christ you will never sin again. I have met people who believed this false doctrine, but they did not get it from the Bible. John writes in chapters one and two, telling Christians how to deal with their sins. He clearly warns us in chapter one of the dangers of saying we have not sinned.

This verse teaches us that as children of God we cannot enjoy sinning, because it breaks our fellowship with Christ. When we abide in Him, it gives us victory over sin. We can live free from the power of sin because we are abiding in Him. If you want to have victory over sin today, then spend as much time as you can thinking about Him, reading His Word, praying to Him, and praising Him with every opportunity you find. When you speak to someone, make a point to bring Him into the conversation. Take the time to thank Him throughout the day for the things He does for you. This is what it means to be abiding in Him.

He has fixed our position in Him through His blood. We are positionally sinless because He is sinless. His sinless life covers our sinful life. This makes us ready subjects for heaven because we are abiding in Christ through what He did on the cross. This is the difference between the saint and the sinner.

The Bible plainly states that sinners have not seen Him and do not know Him. They are not abiding in Him. They have no relationship with Christ, and therefore, they have no fellowship with Christ. Their position has never changed, and they are still lost in their sins. I'm glad I'm abiding in Him, and He is abiding in me. This is the difference between the two.

"A Belief That Behaves"

1 John 3:7 – *"Little children, let no man deceive you: he that doeth righteousness is righteous, even as he is righteous."*

Children can sometimes be easily deceived because of their lack of knowledge. The same is true about those who are spiritually young in the Lord. John is going to establish a truth that every believer must grasp to prevent them from being deceived by false teachers. He wants young believers to realize that we have a belief that behaves.

Find out what someone believes, then you will know how they will behave. There are many today who are living in unrighteousness. They promote their sinful lifestyles and applaud the acts of others who indulge in wickedness. They love their sin because they do not have a new nature. Sinning is the only thing they know to do. I do want to add, that a person is not a sinner because they sin; they sin because they are a sinner. This is a reflection of who they really are inside.

Those who act righteously do so because they have a new nature. Christ living in the believer gives them the ability to live a righteous life. They no longer want to continue in sin, but they have a desire to follow after righteousness. Their belief affects their behavior. What has happened on the inside has produced a change on the outside.

There are a lot of people who claim righteousness, but they live in unrighteousness. Why is this? The answer is very simple. Though they might say they believe the Bible, their life tells us another story. I know a child of God can backslide, but the truth is, many don't believe what they say they do. Their actions speak louder than their words. They are not backsliding, because they have never experienced righteousness a day in their life. They have no desire to live a righteous life. A person who is saved will live a righteous life.

"Jesus Versus Satan"

1 John 3:8 – "He that committeth sin is of the devil; for the devil sinneth from the beginning. For this purpose the Son of God was manifested, that he might destroy the works of the devil."

I'm reminded of the old song, "Who is on the Lord's side?" Before salvation, we were not on His side. We were on the wrong side, the side of sin, Satan, death, and destruction. We were lost without God and without hope. Just like our verse declares, we committed sin and were of the devil. Those who are still in sin and live in sin are of the devil because sin originated with Satan, not God.

I'm glad that this is not the end of the story if you are saved! Those of us who know Christ know that we are not what we used to be. We may still have a sin nature, but thank God, we have a new nature. The Son of God has been manifested in our lives. Through salvation, He gives us victory over our sin and Satan. His purpose in our lives is to deliver us from the devil and make us more like Him.

Every time a sinner is saved, the Son of God destroys the works of the devil. His goal is to drag sinners to hell. The purpose of Calvary is to deliver sinners from hell. This war between God and Satan began in heaven when God kicked Lucifer and those who followed him out of heaven and destined them for hell. The devil then sought out man and used him as the battleground between good and evil. All through the pages of God's Word, the battle is not between Satan and man, but Satan and God. The good news is that God always defeats Satan in His own time. Christ defeated him at Calvary, and we can defeat him through Christ. We read in Revelation that in the end, Christ will defeat him and all who follow him. Friend, if you know Jesus, you are on the winning side! You are on the side that has already won!

"Position and Condition"

1 John 3:9 – *"Whosoever is born of God doth not commit sin; for his seed remaineth in him: and he cannot sin, because he is born of God."*

Every time I read this verse, I think of the beloved evangelist who preached a revival at our church on our position versus our condition. We know that John is not teaching sinless perfection because in chapter one and verse nine, he tells us what a Christian is to do when they sin. John understands that our position cannot change, but our condition is always changing. Our position depends upon Christ, and our condition depends upon us.

Thank the Lord that one of these days our position and our condition will be the same. When this takes place, our position and condition will be glorification. What a day this is going to be! We will no longer struggle with this sinful flesh. The seed that has been planted on the inside is going to blossom forth with glorified life!

A true child of God understands what it means to have this seed living on the inside. We cannot enjoy the pleasures of sin like we once did before we were born again. Our spirit has been alive in Christ, and sin no longer has dominion over us. Even though the flesh is not saved and glorified yet, our position is glorious. The seed living in us gives us the victory we need to continue serving God. I encourage you to take a few moments and reflect on where you were before salvation and where you are now. Think about the old you in contrast to the new you in Christ. If you have been saved, then you can clearly see the difference salvation makes. It changes your position and then begins the immediate work on your condition.

"The Devil's Seed"

1 John 3:10 – *"In this the children of God are manifest, and the children of the devil: whosoever doeth not righteousness is not of God, neither he that loveth not his brother."*

Our text teaches us that there is a clear distinction between the children of God and the children of the devil. One of the biggest lies the devil ever told was that we are all God's children. That is not what the Bible says about being a child of God. We do not become a child of God until we are born again. If you are wondering whose child we were before we got saved, the answer is found in the early verses of Ephesians chapter two. We were a child of wrath. We were the devil's seed, separated from God, living in sin, and following after Satan.

There are two distinctive marks in our verse that reveal the devil's seed. The first mark is that they have no desire to do righteousness. They live according to their own sinful desires. People who are lost have no desire to please God, obey His Word, or do His will. They will do whatever they deem to be right in their own lives. They live by their own standards and rules. Sinners often become self-righteous and full of pride. All of these actions and attitudes are the result of the devil's seed living in them.

The second mark is that they have no genuine love for the brethren. This means that they do not know what true brotherly love is, because it is Christ's love. You cannot express something that you do not possess. I've seen people in church who would rather be with worldly people than with God's people. They acted like a fish out of water at church but came alive when around those who do not profess God. They are more comfortable around the lost than the saved. It is evident as to whom they belong. People don't listen to our lips until they first look at our lives. This tells it all, my friend!

"A Lovely Message"

1 John 3:11 – *"For this is the message that ye heard from the beginning, that we should love one another."*

The admonishment in our text is to love one another. How much better would our world be today if believers practiced this verse daily? When I look at this verse, I see three reasons why we should love one another. Allow me to share them with you briefly.

The first reason is that this is "the message." This is what our verse says to each one of us. This is not John's message, but this is God's message. Every time the Lord gives us a message, we should pay close attention to it and take it seriously.

The second reason is that this message has existed from the beginning. This is not some new message that has not previously been proclaimed. We have a message that can be seen in the Old Testament. When God created man, He taught man how to love. Adam experienced God's love for him as an individual. God then gave Eve to Adam, to share the garden with him. When they sinned that awful day in the garden, they saw and felt God's love and mercy. Throughout the pages of His Word, we read of God's love for man. Christ spoke about His love, then proved it on the cross when He died for our sins.

The final reason we should love one another is that we have one another to love. Think about how God has used the brethren to help strengthen our lives. Where would we be without a good church to attend? What would our lives be like if we had to serve God alone without Christian fellowship? We should never take our brothers and sisters in Christ for granted. May the Lord help us share this message of love to some brother today.

"Why Cain Killed Abel"

1 John 3:12 – *"Not as Cain, who was of that wicked one, and slew his brother. And wherefore slew he him? Because his own works were evil, and his brother's righteous."*

Have you ever wondered why Cain slew his brother? Abel had never attempted to hurt Cain or do him wrong. He was no threat to him; Abel loved Cain. The two of them had grown up, played, worked, and worshipped God together. They shared many precious memories. Then, one day it was all destroyed when Cain slew Abel with a vengeance.

Perhaps, we could offer up several reasons that may prove to be true, but the best answer is in our verse. The Bible tells us why Cain slew Abel. He killed his brother because his own works were evil, and his brother's works were righteous. Abel was living in obedience to God, and Cain was living in disobedience. He envied his brother because he did what God asked him to do.

We live in a world of envy and jealousy. However, envy and jealousy are far uglier when it is seen among the brethren. When a brother turns on his brother, it is a very sad commentary. What a disgrace that he would want to eliminate his brother. Whenever church members and preachers turn against each other, it is just as shameful.

I know misunderstandings happen, but let me remind you that some turn against their brother because they themselves are not doing right. They want others to follow their ways, and when they don't, they are stricken with envy, pride, and jealousy. Evil hates righteousness and always will. We must be careful that we don't allow it in our hearts and let it turn us against our own. Remember, if we live by the sword, we will die by the sword.

"Do Not Be Surprised!"

1 John 3:13 – *"Marvel not, my brethren, if the world hate you. "*

I like the fact that this is a small verse with so much to say. John begins by saying, "marvel not." In plain Georgia language, that means "do not be surprised." Does it ever shock you to see what surprises many Christians today? This verse has that kind of surprise in it.

John is speaking to saved people and tells them not to be surprised if the world hates Christians. This makes perfectly good sense, seeing that the world is the enemy of God. The Bible teaches this in James chapter four. So, if the world is the enemy of our Heavenly Father, then it only stands to reason that it will be the enemy of our Father's children. They hated His Son and willingly put Him to death. He told us that the world would hate us, just as it hated Him. This should come as no surprise, but I will share something with you that will surprise you.

Despite what the Bible says and what they did to Jesus, some believers today still try to win the world's favor. Some believers try to mix the world with Christianity, hoping the world will learn to love them. Compromising our doctrine, conviction, and testimony will not make us popular in the world; it will only make us ineffective.

Paul said that if we live a godly life, they will not only hate us, but they will persecute us. If we love the world, then our love for God diminishes, and we find ourselves on the wrong side. My friend, do not be bothered by what the world says or thinks about you. Be a light in a dark world. Shine for Jesus and hold strong your beliefs. When others compromise, take note that the world does not treat them fairly, and God does not show them favor. I never want to trade the favor of God for a false love of the world. Do not be surprised, just be steadfast.

"A Mark of True Salvation"

1 John 3:14 – *"We know that we have passed from death unto life, because we love the brethren. He that loveth not his brother abideth in death."*

A great study through 1 John would be to research all of the verses that reveal the marks of genuine salvation. After all, that is the reason John is writing this Epistle. Perhaps we will begin that study when we complete this devotional book. Here is one verse that marks true salvation in the life of a believer.

A true child of God will love the brethren. This is not a love that is seen through mere words, but a love that is evident by the believer's actions. When someone gets saved, leaves the old crowd, and joins the church, it gives assurance to other believers. Even when someone has been in church all their life and is religious but lost, their love for the church is different after they are saved. It is no longer about a social gathering but becomes personal because now the church is their family.

I've seen people in church who were lost, even though they regularly attended services, but they were just like people who never went to church at all. They always seemed to be on the outside looking in, even though they were there every service. Something was missing in their life, genuine salvation.

The Bible is clear in this verse; if anyone professes to be saved but has no love for the church, then they are still dead. They are dead to the things of God. A dead man has no life, no desire, no hunger, no understanding, and no love for anything. Dear reader, if this is you, then you do not have the mark of true salvation in your life. This verse will either convince you or condemn you. Think about it, and if you are saved, rejoice; but if you are lost, then trust Christ today as your Savior.

"A Sad Soul"

1 John 3:15 – *"Whosoever hateth his brother is a murderer: and ye know that no murderer hath eternal life abiding in him."*

I would like for us to reflect on the first word of our verse. This is a word that reaches all four corners of the globe and includes each individual soul. The word "whosoever" is a wonderful word when placed in verses like John 5:24, or Romans 10:13. However, when placed in this particular verse, it does not speak of the positive for man but rather the evil.

I would call the "whosoever" in this verse a sad soul for several reasons. I will give them to you shortly, but let me ask "whosoever" is reading this to consider two important things. First, inventory your own soul, and secondly, consider a sad soul such as the one in our text.

This soul is sad because it is filled with hatred. If hatred is dealt with and confessed before God, then the soul can have victory. John is speaking about hatred in the continual sense. When hatred is harbored in the heart, then there can be no joy or peace. The soul becomes cold and miserable.

Another reason is because of who this soul has chosen to hate. He has chosen to hate a brother. Now, brothers can be good or bad. They can treat you right or they can treat you wrong, but at the end of the day, the word "brother" should mean something to all of us. If there is a true family tie, then it should not cause us to hate, but to forgive.

We should consider the degree of hatred that this soul has toward his so-called brother. He hates him to the point that he wants to take his life. Perhaps you say that you have never wanted to murder anyone, but if they died, how would you feel? The final description of this sad soul is that he does not have eternal life. Hatred has kept

him from receiving the treasure of eternal life. Are you this sad soul?
Do you know a sad soul today?

"His Life for Mine"

1 John 3:16 – *"Hereby perceive we the love of God, because he laid down his life for us: and we ought to lay down our lives for the brethren."*

When I look at this verse, I see three key thoughts within it. First, I see a perception; second, a price; and third, a principle. Allow me to share each of these with you for our devotional thought.

First, we consider the perception in the first phrase. The word "perception" means to be aware of or to see. We are aware of the love of God and can see His love for us. For those who are not aware of the love of God, all they need to do is look into the pages of His Word. His Word gives us awareness of how much He really does love fallen man.

Also, we see that Christ paid the ultimate price for every sinner. He gave His life for you and me. He died when we were not aware of it. He died when man did not appreciate it. He died when man did not ask Him to die. I'm glad that He knew what it would take to purchase our salvation. He knew the price and was willing to pay it. He gave His life for mine!

Finally, we are left with a great principle. Just as Christ proved His love for us by laying down His life, we are to do the same for our brethren. You might wonder if any brethren have ever died for you. The answer is yes. Think about the blood of the martyrs of the early church that stood against Rome. Think about the brethren who gave their lives for the Bible to be printed. Think about the Baptists who died so we could put the name on our sign. Think about the Christian countrymen who died so we could have freedom of religion. What a principle that Christians have lived by down through the ages. Where did this dedication of love for each other come from? This principle is real because He gave His life for mine! Remember, if we will not live for Christ, then we will surely not die for Him.

"Stingy Christians?"

1 John 3:17 – *"But whoso hath this world's good, and seeth his brother have need, and shutteth up his bowels of compassion from him, how dwelleth the love of God in him?"*

I do not think the two words that make up the title for this devotional go together. That is why you see the question marks that follow it. From what he has written in this verse, John felt the same way. The truth is, that you cannot be a Christian and live a stingy life. Christianity is all about giving, not keeping. Jesus taught us that in the Gospels. He taught us that it is more blessed to give than to receive. For us to save our life is to lose it, and to lose our life is to save it. The principle is, we get by giving, but notice how much we can keep.

If a child of God is filled with His love, he will have a desire to give. He will also be called on to give. We are not challenged to give out of our plenty, but to give out of our poverty. This means we are to give sacrificially, as we see the need to give. Sacrificial giving is the only kind of giving that God and His Son know. The Father gave the Son, and the Son gave His life, because of His love for us and our need for salvation. What great sacrifices were made for us to be saved.

After becoming a child of God and experiencing His great love, how could we not exhibit the same toward others? How can someone hear the gospel and not give to missions so that others will have the same opportunity they had? How can we have the means to help others and pass them by, when He never passed us by? You might say, "But preacher, I know they have a need, and I have the goods, but the sacrifice is too great for me to make. It will cost me more than I am willing to give." Really? He never said that to you.

His sacrifice was greater. No sacrifice is too much of a sacrifice when dominated by love.

"Love in Action"

1 John 3:18 – *"My little children, let us not love in word, neither in tongue; but in deed and in truth."*

A Christian's love should always be love in action. This is the exhortation in our text. If we say we love, but never put our words into motion, they are just empty words. So many today know how to talk the talk, but do not walk the walk. This is discouraging to other believers, deceptive to the one doing the talking, and nothing but hypocrisy to a lost world. We should note that if a blind world can see through this kind of fake Christianity, then we should never be fooled by it. Words of love with no action might make the one talking feel good, but it does nothing for those in need.

Don't be fooled by smooth talkers. Beware of those who use words of flattery, but never lift a finger to help others along the way. Many people love the spotlight, the platform, and the reputation of being a giver, but in reality, they are just takers. If you think about it, the ones who are always loving in action are normally the ones saying the least about it. They are constantly proving their love by their service. Their love is not announced but is always in motion towards those around them. Do not forget those who have quietly, but steadily, invested in you. But the ones who want to announce their Christian love, do so with little or no service. Real love is more than rhetoric; real love is love in action.

Real love is not only in deed, but it is in truth. Real love doesn't always tell us what we want to hear, but what we need to know. Real love will always be in line with the Word of God. Real love never leads us away from the Truth but leads us further into the Truth. Just because someone says they love you doesn't always mean they do. Their actions will always speak louder than their words. We are given a command in this text to love in action. Make it your goal to put your love for others into action today.

"Has the Truth Taken Root?"

1 John 3:19 – *"And hereby we know that we are of the truth, and shall assure our hearts before him."*

Our salvation is assured by the Word of God, the Work of Christ, and the Witness of the Spirit. The deeds that we do are by no means the foundation of our salvation, but they do assure our hearts that faith has taken root in our lives. It has been said many times that "works do not produce faith, but genuine faith does produce works." The bottom line is when we are truly saved, we will have assurance. There will be a deep, settled peace on the inside that we are born again. We will know that the Truth has taken root!

This entire Epistle gives us nuggets of the Truth that let us know we belong to Him. The Holy Spirit will use the Word of God to convince us within our hearts that we are saved. Now, we know that, according to the Scriptures, our hearts are deceitful and can lead us astray. However, when we fill our hearts with the Word of God and place our faith in the work of Christ, then the Spirit will guide our hearts into the Truth. This is what provides us with this wonderful assurance. There is no greater joy than knowing you are saved.

Those who walk in darkness and deception do so because of one of these two reasons. They have either never heard the Truth, or they have chosen not to believe the Truth. This is why a deceived soul has no assurance within. Those of us who have heard the Truth, and believed the Truth, have a great responsibility to share it with others. We must help them find the same peace that we have found. Ask yourself today, do you have that assurance in your heart? Has the Truth taken root in your heart? If the answer is yes, then share the Truth with someone today. You never know when it is going to take root in some lost soul that is searching.

"God is Greater"

1 John 3:20 – *"For if our heart condemn us, God is greater than our heart, and knoweth all things."*

No matter how hard we try, we do not live up to our own expectations, let alone God's. The same heart that can assure us, as we read in the previous verse, can also fill us with guilt. Our hearts can condemn us to the point that we live in defeat. This proves a very important principle for every believer. The heart is not to be ignored, but it is not to be the final authority either.

Fact, faith, and feelings are how we are to operate. The facts of God's Word tell me the Truth. Faith in the Word of God gives me assurance in the Truth. After all, truth does no good if we choose not to believe it. Then, feelings are a part of what we have heard and believe. The only problem with this is that sometimes feelings can be misleading.

The heart can condemn us for our shortcomings and failures. This is not a bad thing; it is a good thing. We should feel condemned in our hearts when we sin, come up short or fail. Condemnation can lead us to repentance and victory.

Whenever we repent, we must not allow our hearts to rule us. God is greater than how we feel. Many Christians live defeated lives because they trust the feelings of their hearts over the facts of God's Word. Whenever I come up short, God's Word says if I'll confess it and forsake it, I'm forgiven. If I have trusted and obeyed the Word, then no matter how my heart makes me feel, God is greater than my heart. My assurance is not in how I feel, but rather in what the Word says. We must not let our hearts be the final authority but allow His Word to be the final authority in our lives. God is greater than any sin we can commit. God is greater than any mistake we can make. God is greater than any sorrow we might bear. God is greater!

"The Secret Chambers of the Heart"

1 John 3:21 – *"Beloved, if our heart condemn us not, then have we confidence toward God."*

We have come to the third devotional emphasizing the heart. In verse nineteen, the first devotional showed us the confirmation of the heart. In verse twenty, the second devotional dealt with the condemnation of the heart. Our devotional here, in verse twenty-one, shows the confidence within the heart. Together, these three verses prove that God works in the secret chambers of man's heart.

The Truths of God's Word take root in man's heart, producing faith-giving assurance. God is greater than the heart of man, so when the heart condemns what God has already forgiven, we can lean on His Word, His work, and His witness. Then God uses the secret chamber of man's heart to produce the confidence we need toward Him.

God not only puts His Word in our hearts, but He places His will in our hearts. His salvation, His Scriptures, and His Spirit give us confidence in our hearts toward Him. He also gives us the confidence and the courage to move forward for His glory. The Bible tells us in Colossians 3:23, that whatever we do for God should be from our heart. The secret chamber of man's heart is where his true motive dwells.

Whenever we do wrong or allow sin into our lives, it always affects our hearts first. Sin causes us to lose heart for God and His will for our life. We may still be active in service, but our hearts are not in it. When this happens, our confidence in God's approval for our lives is no longer there. Our hearts are condemning us and telling us something is not right. Again, the secret chambers of our hearts can only be seen by God. He will reveal to us what dwells inside, and He can convict, cleanse, and give us the confidence we need to serve Him.

"Prayers in Shoe Leather"

1 John 3:22 – *"And whatsoever we ask, we receive of him, because we keep his commandments, and do those things that are pleasing in his sight."*

I remember hearing an old black preacher say, "You've got to pray and work, and work and pray. When work won't get it, prayer will, and when prayer won't get it, work will. And when neither prayer nor work will get it, you forget it, because you didn't need it anyhow." The preacher's statement best describes our verse for today. We are encouraged to pray and perform.

If you are praying to be a better soul-winner, then you must also pass out tracts and witness. If you are praying for your Sunday School class to grow, then you must invite more people to attend. God will not do what He has given us the ability to do. Praying does not relieve us from doing our part.

Just because a husband is praying for his wife to be healed does not mean he stops taking her to the doctor. He should seek all the medical assistance he can, while he prays for her healing. God may heal her without any medical help, or He may use the doctors and modern medicine to heal her from her sickness. The husband must ask and do until the answer comes.

God answers the prayers of those who obey His commandments and do what is pleasing in His sight. I hear a lot of people talking about praying, but when you look at the way they live, I'm doubtful God hears their prayers. They may be saved, but they are disobedient in the way they are living. How we live does affect our prayer life. Christians are not perfect, but they are forgiven. They can see the mighty hand of God working in their lives if they will seek Him. Remember, the next time you pray about something, keep on working while you are waiting for an answer. Put your prayers in shoe leather by doing all you can in the situation. Be assured that when you have done all you can, He will do the rest!

"Follow His Command"

1 John 3:23 – "And this is his commandment, That we should believe on the name of his Son Jesus Christ, and love one another, as he gave us commandment."

God publicly announced His approval of His Son at Jesus' baptism and again on the Mount of Transfiguration. These two incidents are not the only times that we see God's approval on His Son, but they would have been enough to convince anyone that Jesus was the Son of God.

Faith in Jesus Christ is essential for man to have a right relationship with God. You cannot know God without knowing His Son, Jesus Christ. Many cults have been created as a form of false religion. They all declare the same damnable heresy. They teach men that they can have a relationship with a god, or the True God, without believing in Jesus Christ. We must follow His command to put our trust in Christ alone.

Jesus also gave believers the command to love one another. A true believer will be obedient to both of these commands. They will believe in Jesus Christ and love other believers. This comes naturally for a saved person, but it is foreign to a lost person.

My concern is for the untold numbers who profess to be saved, but they trust in themselves rather than Christ. They think their good works or religious accomplishments are enough to get them to heaven. Just because someone knows the lingo and is familiar with the format of Christianity does not mark them as a true believer. Love must be the overwhelming mark of genuine salvation. This same crowd finds it difficult to get along with pastors, preachers, and other members of the church. Christians love the Savior and have a love for one another. If you find it difficult to follow His commandment of love, then do an inventory in your heart today.

"Who's Living Inside of You?"

1 John 3:24 – "And he that keepeth his commandments dwelleth in him, and he in him. And hereby we know that he abideth in us, by the Spirit which he hath given us."

This would seem to be a strange title to a lost soul, but not to those who have been redeemed. As the songwriter said, "Never alone, no, never alone, He promised never to leave me, never to leave me alone." What a great promise to the child of God! When we accept Christ as our Savior, John tells us that His Spirit abides in us.

My question for you, dear reader, is, "Who's living inside of you?" Are you alone without Christ? Do you not have the Spirit living within you? It is impossible to be saved and possess His Spirit in your heart and not know it.

Believers are indwelt with the Spirit, but they are also to walk in the Spirit and be filled with the Spirit. We do this by keeping His commandments. Keeping His commandments keeps sin out of our lives and allows the Spirit of God to lead us. There is no greater joy than when we are abiding in Him and letting the Spirit control us.

Whenever the Spirit controls our lives, He brings peace and joy. The Spirit gives us wisdom and guidance for daily living. The Spirit empowers us for service when we yield to Him. The Spirit also gives us great assurance that we belong to Christ. What a privilege it is that we don't have to be alone. I'm so glad we have His presence living on the inside. If you are one to doubt or struggle with your salvation, then allow the Spirit of God to settle it for you. He will either convict or convince you of your need. If He is living on the inside, He will make Himself known to you. If He is not living on the inside, He will let you know that as well. It is never the job of the Holy Spirit to cause confusion. Get into His Word, and seek His guidance, and He will bring you to the knowledge of the Truth.

1 John 4

1 Beloved, believe not every spirit, but try the spirits whether they are of God: because many false prophets are gone out into the world.

2 Hereby know ye the Spirit of God: Every spirit that confesseth that Jesus Christ is come in the flesh is of God:

3 And every spirit that confesseth not that Jesus Christ is come in the flesh is not of God: and this is that spirit of antichrist, whereof ye have heard that it should come; and even now already is it in the world.

4 Ye are of God, little children, and have overcome them: because greater is he that is in you, than he that is in the world.

5 They are of the world: therefore speak they of the world, and the world heareth them.

6 We are of God: he that knoweth God heareth us; he that is not of God heareth not us. Hereby know we the spirit of truth, and the spirit of error.

7 Beloved, let us love one another: for love is of God; and every one that loveth is born of God, and knoweth God.

8 He that loveth not knoweth not God; for God is love.

9 In this was manifested the love of God toward us, because that God sent his only begotten Son into the world, that we might live through him.

10 Herein is love, not that we loved God, but that he loved us, and sent his Son to be the propitiation for our sins.

11 Beloved, if God so loved us, we ought also to love one another.

12 No man hath seen God at any time. If we love one another, God dwelleth in us, and his love is perfected in us.

13 Hereby know we that we dwell in him, and he in us, because he hath given us of his Spirit.

14 And we have seen and do testify that the Father sent the Son to be the Saviour of the world.

15 Whosoever shall confess that Jesus is the Son of God, God dwelleth in him, and he in God.

16 And we have known and believed the love that God hath to us. God is love; and he that dwelleth in love dwelleth in God, and God in him.

17 Herein is our love made perfect, that we may have boldness in the day of judgment: because as he is, so are we in this world.

18 There is no fear in love; but perfect love casteth out fear: because fear hath torment. He that feareth is not made perfect in love.

19 We love him, because he first loved us.

20 If a man say, I love God, and hateth his brother, he is a liar: for he that loveth not his brother whom he hath seen, how can he love God whom he hath not seen?

21 And this commandment have we from him, That he who loveth God love his brother also.

"Spiritual Error"

1 John 4:1 – *"Beloved, believe not every spirit, but try the spirits whether they are of God: because many false prophets are gone out into the world."*

John opens this chapter with compassion. He does this by using the word "beloved." This word reveals his love for those he is speaking to. I'm sure you have heard the saying, "No one cares how much you know until they know how much you care." John first shows us that he cares.

We also see John's caution, as he begins to point out his purpose for writing this text. He wants to caution these new converts not to believe every spirit they come in contact with. We should always note the spirit in which someone is preaching, teaching, or testifying. We cannot afford to be easily influenced or swayed by the personalities and charisma of men.

He now gives a command concerning spiritual error. How can we avoid it? How do we know if it is the Holy Spirit or false doctrine by a seducing spirit? John commands us to try the spirits to see whether they are of God. The question in my mind is, how do we try the spirits? We try the spirits by the Truth of God's Word. His Truth will always reveal man's error, and His Spirit will always line up with His Word. The Bible is our standard and guide for all that we believe.

John has revealed his compassion, his caution, and his command, but he closes this verse with his cause. Why should we be so particular when it comes to what we read and who we listen to in this world? He tells us that there are many false prophets in this world. If you know the Truth of God's Word today, you should rejoice. We shout and share God's Word to all because we have the Truth! Thank God we are not living our lives in spiritual error!

"Is That God or Not?"

1 John 4:2 – "Hereby know ye the Spirit of God: Every spirit that confesseth that Jesus Christ is come in the flesh is of God:"

One of the things I love most about the Bible is that it gives us clear instructions on how to make the right choices. The first verse of this chapter warned us about spiritual error. The second verse teaches us how to know if what we are seeing and hearing is God or not. I'm thankful we do not have to be deceived, but we learn from God's Word what is true and what is false.

We can know if a man, a message, or a ministry is of God. We can also know when it is not of God. John emphasizes that in this first phrase, by reassuring us that there is one principle that will tell us if it is of God. The Spirit of God will always speak of Jesus Christ. This means that everything will be built upon Jesus, and everything will magnify Jesus. Whenever the emphasis is upon anything other than Christ, it is not of God.

Do not allow the personalities and philosophies of man to persuade you. Do not follow a ministry that places more emphasis on the Holy Spirit than on Jesus Christ. The Spirit of God speaks of Jesus Christ and not of Himself. The Spirit of God declares Jesus Christ to be God in the flesh. This is what separates Christianity from all other religions. We preach and believe that Jesus Christ came into this world and lived a sinless life. We believe that the Bible proclaims Him to be the God-man! He was the perfect Son of God, who lived a sinless life in the flesh for thirty-three and a half years. We believe that Jesus Christ is alive at the right hand of the Father and that He is the only begotten Son of God.

Friends, remember that the Spirit of God and the Word of God will always magnify Jesus. The Spirit will reveal Christ to a lost world, and so should we.

"Four Fundamental Facts"

1 John 4:3 – *"And every spirit that confesseth not that Jesus Christ is come in the flesh is not of God: and this is that spirit of antichrist, whereof ye have heard that it should come; and even now already is it in the world."*

I want us to see four fundamental facts in this verse. What you and I will notice about these facts is that they are practical, proven, and relevant for the days we are living in. John is talking in this chapter about what is true and what is false, what is right and what is wrong, what is real and what is not, what is of God and what is of Satan. In a world that is full of confusion and deception, it is a blessing to have the facts of God's Word to stand upon. I'm amazed at how much instruction we receive from the Bible, but I am even more amazed at how much we can receive from just one verse of Scripture.

Fact #1: Any spirit that does not teach that Jesus Christ is come in the flesh is not of God. How simple it is to understand this fact. Those who do not proclaim the Jesus of the Bible are not of God!

Fact #2: The denial of Jesus Christ coming in the flesh is the spirit of the antichrist. Some deny that He was born of a virgin. They deny the deity of Christ and even His existence. We know for a fact this is the working of Satan.

Fact #3: We have heard that it should come. The Bible has warned that scoffers would come, and they have. This proves the accuracy of our Bible.

Fact #4: This kind of spirit is already in the world. Bible students are not surprised nor shaken by those who deny the existence of Jesus in the flesh. The Word of God has taught us that this anti-spirit is already here. What blessed instruction from one verse to help stabilize us during these days.

"Greatness From Within"

1 John 4:4 – "*Ye are of God, little children, and have overcome them: because greater is he that is in you, than he that is in the world.*"

Whenever I read this verse, I cannot help but break it down phrase by phrase. The first thing I notice is our standing. John said, "Ye are of God." This is enough to make us stop and rejoice; we are of God and not of the devil anymore! What a blessed position. Calvary did more than save our souls from hell. Calvary gave us a new standing with God.

The second thing I notice is our size. John used the phrase "little children." This should help remove any pride that might try to creep into our lives. Little children are dependent upon others. They are unable to take care of themselves or do for themselves. They require constant teaching and supervision. This is who we are as believers. The songwriter said it best when he wrote the words, "Lord, I can't even walk without you holding my hand." Like a child, we need His care and guidance.

The third thing I see is our success. John declares that we have "overcome them." For us to have any victory or success in our lives is nothing short of a miracle. How is this possible? How can it be that you and I have overcome error and corruption? How can we win over Satan?

The answer is in the next phrase, where I see the Spirit. John says, "Greater is He that is in you." Our greatness comes from within. This greatness has nothing to do with self, but everything to do with the Spirit. The victorious Christian life is one in which a believer is filled with the Holy Spirit.

Finally, I see Satan. John talks about "he that is in the world." The Devil is a defeated foe. He can have no victory apart from us giving it to him. If you are saved, greatness is living within you. The

Spirit will guide us and help us to conquer the world, the flesh, and the Devil.

"As the World Turns"

1 John 4:5 – *"They are of the world: therefore speak they of the world, and the world heareth them."*

I remember as a child, an old soap opera that came on television entitled "As the World Turns." I had no interest in the show because of my age and the nature of the show itself. I do remember that it was full of filth and drama. There was nothing decent, wholesome, or godly about the series. It was a daily show filled with lies, cheating, and deceit. As bad as the television series was, it did reveal what was true about the world we live in today.

As this world turns, it is full of lying, cheating, deceiving, filth, and drama. Our verse mentions the word "world" three times. This verse tells us that false teachers and deceivers are of this world. They speak of the world, and they have the world's ear. The world is listening to them. Have you noticed how the world flocks to someone starting a false doctrine or teaching? On the other hand, the world despises and rejects the truth of the Bible. They turn a deaf ear to the very Book that can rescue them. Why is this? Why is it more inviting for the world to believe a lie?

The answer is in the first phrase of our verse. The world loves false teachers because they are of the world. They speak the world's language. This means there is no righteousness or reproof in their message. So the world listens to what they have to say.

As this world turns, it becomes darker and more deceptive. You and I must continue to give out the truth of God's Word. We must do our best to shine as lights in this world. May God help us to make our lives a light, shining out in the night, to some poor sinner searching for the truth.

"Who Are You Listening To?"

1 John 4:6 – *"We are of God: he that knoweth God heareth us; he that is not of God heareth not us. Hereby know we the spirit of truth, and the spirit of error."*

Who you listen to determines a lot about the decisions you will make in life. Influence is a very powerful tool in today's society. Many have been led astray because they have listened to the wrong individual. It is sobering to think that even the Bible, in the hands of a false teacher, can lead people astray. Though they may have the Truth in their hand, if it is not in their heart, they can become quite dangerous as teachers.

John is bold to declare that he and his fellow laborers are of God and that those who know God will follow and listen to them. Those who are not willing to follow their teaching are not of God. The truth will either bring you closer to the one teaching it, or it will drive you away. This depends on whether or not you have the Spirit of Truth living inside of you. The Holy Spirit confirms truth when it is being taught. He also sends up a red flag when false doctrine is being taught.

Think about the church world today. Consider the masses of people who are flocking to buildings and listening to men who tell them what they want to hear, rather than what they need to hear. They make fun of those who have stood with conviction and preached the truth without apology. They teach a watered-down gospel, portray a nightclub atmosphere in their services, and never say anything that is confrontational or places demands on the listeners. How could anyone who is saved and knows the truth believe that this is right? The answer is they cannot. There is no doubt that many are deceived, but there is one thing that is for sure, a saved person with the Spirit of Truth living in them will know that it is in error. When we go to

Sunday School and church, we should ask ourselves the question, "Who am I listening to?"

"The Cords of Love"

1 John 4:7 – *"Beloved, let us love one another: for love is of God; and every one that loveth is born of God, and knoweth God."*

The verse before us begins by addressing the saints of God. John uses the word "Beloved." How fitting this word is for this verse because it is a word of love, and John is going to emphasize four truths concerning love. I call these cords of love because they seemingly tie together.

The first cord I see is the sharing of love. John gives the admonishment to love one another. Although at times some people can be more challenging to love than others, it is natural for a saint to love other saints. There is a kindred spirit that draws us closer together. True believers have a desire to share brotherly love.

The second cord I see is the source of love. How are we to love total strangers who claim to know God? The answer is simple; it is because we have the love of God in our hearts. Romans 5:5 tells us, "the love of God is shed abroad in our hearts by the Holy Ghost." God gives His children the ability to love one another.

The third cord I see is the security of love. John tells us that everyone who is born of God will have this love. We will love the church, the Bible, the singing, the praising, and the teaching. We love the things of God because we know God. Love is evidence of salvation.

The final cord I see is the strength of love. Love causes us to know God more and more. The more we know of God, the more we love Him. Daily devotions and prayer draw us closer to God and allow us to know Him more on a personal level. They strengthen our relationship with Him and help us to know His will and live in a way that pleases Him. These are the cords of love that bind us together and bind us to our Master.

"The Missing Link"

1 John 4:8 – *"He that loveth not knoweth not God; for God is love."*

How can people live with the absence of love? They never express love for their children, their spouse, or their parents, who sacrificed for them and raised them. What a tragedy when someone lives such a selfish life, only thinking about number one. It is hard to comprehend how someone can abandon their loved ones or go so far as to even mistreat them. Why do we live in a world that at times can seem so cruel?

The answer is in our verse. The Bible makes it clear that God is love, and those who have true love know God. People who have no love do not know Him. God is the missing link in their lives. This is why they do the evil things they do and say the awful things they say. God makes the difference by placing His love within us, and it forever changes us.

We understand why the world is so dangerous today. There is so much hatred and malice on every hand because they do not know the love of God. Think about those who are religious but lost. They are miserable in their religion like a sinner who is miserable in their sin. Again, the missing link is the love of God. This is not a worldly love for passions or self-pleasure, but unconditional spiritual love from the Heavenly Father.

God's love is a love that changes the individual from within. What we see on the outside is an expression of what is happening on the inside. A man who has not experienced this amazing love has not experienced the God of this love. Ask yourself this question, "Do I truly love the things of God?" Here is another question that is even more important: "Do I truly love God?" If you know Him, the answer to both of these questions is "yes." If the answer is "no, I do not love

God nor the things of God," then it means that you do not know God. Those who know Him also love Him.

"Oh, What Love Divine!"

1 John 4:9 – *"In this was manifested the love of God toward us, because that God sent his only begotten Son into the world, that we might live through him."*

When I read our verse, many precious songs flood my mind. Songs like "Amazing Love How Can It Be?", "The Love of God", or "Isn't the Love of Jesus Something Wonderful?". These are all songs that try to describe the divine love given to us. The truth is that the love manifested by God, the Father, and God, the Son, will always be a mystery to those who receive it.

The world may question whether God truly loves them or not, but our verse teaches that God's love was manifested to us. His love is seen through his Son. The Father sent His Son to prove how much He loved us. He was also willing to sacrifice His Son to prove how much He loved us. He greatly manifested His love through Christ, both in life and in death. There has never been a greater display of true love than what can be seen at Calvary.

Another great truth in our verse is that Jesus is the Father's only begotten Son. God gave the only Son He had for you and me. I don't know a parent living who would give one of their children for sinful men, especially if they only had one. All I can say is, "Oh, what love divine!" This is love beyond human comprehension. We should serve Him because we love Him and because He first loved us.

The final thought in our verse is what His love produces. We have all stood by the bedside of a loved one and watched them die. We weep and mourn because we love them. Yet no matter how much we love them, we cannot make them live a second longer. Our love cannot produce life for those whom we love. But, oh, what love divine, that God's love for man, through Jesus Christ, produces life for all who trust and believe. This is love divine!

"The Mystery of His Love"

1 John 4:10 – *"Herein is love, not that we loved God, but that he loved us, and sent his Son to be the propitiation for our sins."*

One of the great mysteries of God's love is that He loved us first. God did not turn His heart toward us because we sought after Him; He took the initiative in our lives. God saw the need in man's life before man was aware that he even had a need. God knew the end result of man and what his eternal state would be if he were not delivered. He knew that man had nothing to offer God within himself. God knew that for man to properly love Him, He would have to put His own love in man's heart. It is such a mystery that God took the initiative to do all of this for us. You might ask yourself, "Why would God do all of this for me?" The answer is very simple; He did it because He loves you.

Think back to a time when you did not love God. Remember how you lived and what your attitude was like. Consider how sinful and shameful your life was at that moment. Now consider this thought, God loved you as much then as He does right now. He has always loved you. Even in those times when you and I had no love for Him, he loved us. What a mystery!

You might be someone who would say, "I grew up in church around the things of God, and I've always loved the church, His Word, and His people." Let me help you by saying that you never really knew how to love any of those things until you were saved and experienced His love. Another thing to consider is that you can love the things of God and not love God Himself. You can love the fellowship with people, the religious works, actions, and gatherings, and still not have a personal relationship with God. When you experience the love of God, you will love those things even more. You will love them because they are about Him and for Him, and not about you and for you. The mystery of God's great love is that He first loved us.

"It Just Makes Sense"

1 John 4:11 – *"Beloved, if God so loved us, we ought also to love one another."*

Heaven will be a place of no misunderstandings. There will be no division or separation in the glory world. It is going to be a place of eternal happiness and love among the family of God. What a time God's people will experience as we live together and serve our Creator and our King!

However, we are not in heaven right now. God's children need each other more in this present world than ever before. Too often, Satan gets the advantage because the brethren allow circumstances and things to come between them. The devil works constantly to try to divide saints and cause ungodly feelings in their hearts toward each other. Think about how much greater the work of God would be today if saints would come together and resolve their differences.

The reason we don't see this happening is because of the pride and pressure among the brethren. If you and I are not careful, we can adopt the schoolyard mentality of choosing sides or showing love to a certain brother or sister based on what others have said about them. The truth of our text is that it just makes sense, that if God would love someone as rotten as you and me, then we ought to show the same love toward others.

So, what if they trample your love or spurn your love? Did we not treat the love of God this same way? We are most like God when we show love, and we are most like Satan when we show hatred or bitterness. I've never had anyone treat me any worse than I've treated Him. We don't like to discuss it, but the fact is that God loves man in spite of himself, and not because of himself. It just makes sense that if someone as Holy and Righteous as God could love someone as wicked and sinful as us, then we can surely love others.

We can especially love our brothers and sisters in Christ. It just makes sense.

"When the Invisible Becomes Visible"

1 John 4:12 – *"No man hath seen God at any time. If we love one another, God dwelleth in us, and his love is perfected in us."*

Atheists will say that God does not exist. They will say that they do not believe in His existence because no one has ever actually seen God. They will also argue that even if He did exist, it would be impossible for Him to be everywhere at the same time. Yet, they believe in something as simple as the air they breathe. Air is not visible, but we know it exists. Air is everywhere at the same time, and it is not something that you can physically see, even though it is right in front of you. Air is important for every human life, for without air, we will cease to live. Air is nothing more than a testimony to the existence of the One who created it. I want to be clear to the reader that God is more real than the air we breathe, and that we need Him more.

Our verse teaches us that no man has seen God, but through brotherly love, He can be seen. He can be known to a cold world that does not know His love. On a cold winter day, you can stand outside and see the air coming out of your mouth or nostrils. The extreme temperature causes the invisible to become visible. This world does not need to see us, but they need to see the love of God in the lives of believers toward one another.

I'm reminded of the night in a local restaurant after church when the waiter approached me. He invited me to his house that night to talk to him and his family about the Bible. I was able to give the family the Gospel that night and pray with them. I asked the gentleman what had prompted him to invite me over at such an hour. He said, "I have been watching you and your members come in and fellowship. My family and I want to have the love that you all have for each other." He said, "I told my wife that it must be a love from

110

above." At that moment, I realized the invisible had been made visible!

"Oh, What a Gift!"

1 John 4:13 – *"Hereby know we that we dwell in him, and he in us, because he hath given us of his Spirit."*

The verse before us holds a triple blessing within it. The first blessing we see is the fact that we can dwell in Him. When you consider who we are, and you consider who He is, then you will realize what a blessing it is to dwell in Him. What a blessing that God would open His heart to us, allowing us to love Him, worship Him, and fellowship with Him. The word "dwell" also reveals the permanence of this relationship.

The second blessing is that He dwells within us. God has a desire to fellowship and walk with us. Our relationship with Him is not one-sided. The Creator of the universe wants to have close communion with us today.

The third blessing in our verse tells us how this is possible. He has given us His Spirit. God knew that we could not get to Him by ourselves, and even if somehow we could, we would not be able to maintain a right relationship with Him. The Scriptures tell us that His thoughts and ways are higher than ours. So, He gave us the greatest gift a believer could ever possess, and that is His Spirit.

The Spirit of God in the life of the believer is the full assurance of salvation. He is a comforter, a companion, a counselor, and a conscience in our lives. What a gift from heaven! I want to challenge you to be sensitive to His presence today. Take the time to hear His voice, and yield to His leadership in your life. Tune out the noise of this world, and the influences around you, and listen to what He has to say to you. Open your Bible, and allow this heavenly gift to work in your life.

"The Heartbeat of God"

1 John 4:14 – *"And we have seen and do testify that the Father sent the Son to be the Saviour of the world."*

What is it that makes the God of the Bible separate from all of the false gods of this world? There are many ways we could answer this question, but I want to answer it by saying, it is because HE IS ALIVE! The God of the Bible is not dead! He is living, breathing, and working in the lives of men. The God of heaven and earth has a heartbeat! Our devotional verse reveals His heartbeat in three distinctive areas.

The first area His heartbeat can be seen is in the souls of men. John says that they have seen and do testify. We know God is alive because His people are alive. The songwriter said, "You ask me how I know He lives, He lives within my heart." If God were dead, His followers would be dead also. The joy of salvation is watching a dead sinner come alive in Christ Jesus.

The second area we can see His heartbeat is in the sacrifice He made by sending His son. God gave His Son for sinful men. All of the other false gods of this world can give nothing. Their religion requires man to give sacrificially for them, while our God sacrificially gave for us. He is only able to give because He is alive. A dead man can give nothing because he has no ability to give. He sees, hears, and feels nothing. Our Creator can see us at all times. He is willing to listen to our prayers and can be touched by our situations in life. He has a heartbeat.

The final area in our verse that declares His heartbeat is His Son. God gave His Son on the cross of Calvary to be the Savior of the world. The heartbeat of God is Jesus. The Father loves the Son, yet He loved us enough to give His Son for us. He gave us His heart when He gave us Jesus. The heartbeat of God is that He wants souls to accept His sacrifice, in giving His Son for them.

"The Door Is Open"

1 John 4:15 – *"Whosoever shall confess that Jesus is the Son of God, God dwelleth in him, and he in God."*

In our devotional verse today, the Lord opens the door for every man. This open door is found in the first word, "whosoever." This is a familiar word in the Scriptures, and is a word that our Savior used often. What a declaration, and what an invitation for all who will accept Christ as their personal Savior! The good news of the Gospel is that everyone, and anyone, can walk through the doorway of salvation. Salvation is an open door!

When I think about the door of salvation, I think about the blessedness of being saved. God does not discriminate when it comes to being born again. This door is open, no matter who you are or what you have done. Every child of God should take a moment to reflect on the blessedness of being born again. Think of the joy you have in knowing Jesus and remember the day you walked through that door.

Those who walk through the door of salvation will surely confess Jesus Christ. Born-again believers tell others about the Savior. They have a desire to share the Gospel of the open door and want others to experience the peace of the Spirit within their lives. If you are saved, then you know what I am talking about. Believers are never alone once they walk through that door, because He lives within them.

There are many who profess to be saved but never mention the name of Jesus. They also don't want you to mention Him to them. There is something wrong with someone who says they are saved, but they don't want to talk about the God that supposedly dwells within their heart. If you know someone like that today, pray for them to be enlightened. I want to encourage you to share this open door with someone today. Find a "whosoever" and help them get through the door!

"His Love Lights the Way for Me"

1 John 4:16 – *"And we have known and believed the love that God hath to us. God is love; and he that dwelleth in love dwelleth in God, and God in him."*

John has had so much to say about love in this Epistle. He has emphasized it over and over again. He has talked about God's love toward us, and our love toward God. Here in our verse, he is doing the same thing again. He will mention it even more as we continue through the book.

Why does he place so much emphasis on this subject? Our verse tells us that it is because God is love. God has given us His love! Just like John, we should never get over this amazing truth. The fact that He loves us should overwhelm us to the point that we want to talk about it often.

Another reason why John mentions the subject of love so much is because love leads to life! God's love for us has given us His Son and has brought new life to us in Christ. We will see that more clearly in the verses to come. The greatest gift from God to us is His Son. This gift is a result of His love for man.

His love lives within us and causes us to live in Him. God's love has brought about this wonderful relationship and has given us both life and light for the journey. It reminds me of the old song that we sing, "His Love Lights the Way for Me." How true this is, dear reader? His love gives us salvation, and His love will give us direction until we reach His throne above. He has promised to guard us and guide us every step of the journey.

Take the time today to enjoy the love God has given you. Do not forget that He cares for you, and He is there, ready to help you with the struggles of life. Allow His love to light your pathway and guide you in every decision. He has your best interest in mind and desires to lead you in the light.

"Boldness on Judgment Day?"

1 John 4:17 – "Herein is our love made perfect, that we may have boldness in the day of judgment: because as he is, so are we in this world."

There are a lot of future events that I look forward to in eternity, but I have to be honest that there is one I greatly dread. I both fear and dread that great judgment morning. Standing before the Creator and giving an account for the deeds I have done and the life I have lived is not something I'm looking forward to when I leave this world.

The Bible says that we can have boldness in the day of judgment. Doesn't that sound strange in light of a day that looks so dreadful? The confidence that we can have on that day is not in us but in Christ. We can have boldness in Him! We can have boldness in what He has done for us and through us. We can also have boldness in the fact that He loves us, and that love will be complete on judgment day.

Think about how parents deal with their children. They see all, hear all, and know all when it comes to their little ones. They know the faults and failures, and the many shortcomings of their child. They remember the times that they have been disappointed by them. A parent knows more about that child than any investigator or court of law could ever bring up. However, when all is said and done, the parents still love them and will deal with them out of love. The child can stand before them with boldness, knowing that love will rule over them.

The same is true about a bridegroom and his bride. He may know all of her imperfections and mistakes, but love gives the bride boldness that she can stand before him despite her imperfections. On judgment day, our love will be made perfect as we stand before the throne with boldness, understanding that the One who will judge us is the One who loves us with an eternal love. He will judge righteously with a heart of love!

"The Power of Love"

1 John 4:18 – "There is no fear in love; but perfect love casteth out fear: because fear hath torment. He that feareth is not made perfect in love."

Fear is an emotion that every individual has to face. No one likes to live in fear, but we all know what it's like to have to deal with it. Our verse has a lot to say about this subject. I want you to examine with me four fundamental truths about fear.

First, notice the truth about fear. The Bible says, "There is no fear in love." A child who knows that his parents love him does not live in fear of them, nor does a wife live in fear of her husband when she knows he loves her. There is no fear in love.

The second thing I see is the triumph over fear. Why is there no fear in love? The reason is that love casts it out. Love conquers fear and removes it from the equation. We know that those who love you would never intentionally harm you. We understand that they have your best interest in mind. If this is true with man, how much more with our Heavenly Father.

The third thing we see is the torment of fear. Think about how fear can control an individual's life. Fear can create misery and bring defeat. Fear can bring sadness and sorrow to a life that used to be filled with joy and peace. Fear can cause someone to destroy their life and even the lives of others.

The fourth and last thing we see is the trickery of fear. You see, fear itself has no power. Fear is nothing more than an emotion, and most of the time it is not even a reality. A child of God who lives in fear of their future has chosen to trade love for fear. The more we love God, and walk in His Word, the more we overcome fear. Our love for God grows as we grow and fear diminishes from our lives. Trade your fears for love, believing that God cares for you. Do not allow the trickery of fear to rob you of the power of love.

"True Love"

1 John 4:19 – *"We love him, because he first loved us."*

    I'm always amazed at how the Bible can say so much in one phrase or verse. This is a simple, but profound, text when we consider it. If we are not careful, we can read it and not truly take in all that it has to say to us.

    First, think about the reverse in this verse. The first phrase declares that we love Him. Can you truly say that today? Do you love Christ? If the answer is yes, then pause for a moment and consider the time that you did not love Him. Think about when you went through life and never considered God. Maybe you had the attitude that you wanted nothing to do with Him. Look at how things have been reversed in your life! Now you love Him and desire to have a relationship with Him. This is a great miracle in your life.

    Second, think about the reason why we love Him. The Bible uses the word "because." This word tells us that we don't just love Him, but that there is a reason why we love Him. Let me say that there are a lot of reasons why we love Him. There are more reasons than we could ever list on paper. He gives us reasons every day to love Him more and more. When we consider His salvation, His blessings, His protection, His provision, and His promises, how could we not love Him? When we think about His person, we love HIM!

    Finally, there is the reality in this verse. The reality is that He first loved us! He loved us before He created us, and He loved us before He saved us. God has always loved us. The reason we love Him is that He first loved us. If God had not loved us enough to send us His Son, we would have never loved Him. If He had not loved us enough to send us His Word, and His Spirit, we would have never loved Him. The songwriter said that "He is the reason why we love

Him so." I'm so glad that God took the initiative and loved us when we were unlovable. This is true love at its best!

"Removing the Mask"

1 John 4:20 – *"If a man say, I love God, and hateth his brother, he is a liar: for he that loveth not his brother whom he hath seen, how can he love God whom he hath not seen?"*

I want you to think about the first phrase of our verse today, "If a man say." People will say a lot of things but just because someone says something that doesn't make it true. The Bible teaches us here that if a man says one thing, but his life doesn't back it up, then he is a liar. You cannot say you love God and hate your brother. Saying that something is so, does not make it so.

Think about the man in our text. I think the man is saved because the verse declares that he has a brother in Christ. The Bible is clear in the phrase "loveth not HIS brother." You cannot have a brother without being a brother. The truth is that he may be saved, but he is a hypocrite and an imposter. He is saying he has a right relationship with God, but he does not have a right relationship with his brother. The Bible calls this man a liar.

This man needs to remove the mask of religious pride and hypocrisy. He needs to get real about himself, his relationship with God, and the broken fellowship he has in his heart toward a brother. How much stronger and thriving would our churches be today if God's children would exercise this principle? We could have revival if only believers would lay aside feelings and differences and restore relationships with each other.

The mask must first be removed. If you have something in your heart toward another believer, then make it right today. This will hinder your walk with God. No matter what you say, the Bible is clear that you can't love God, whom you cannot see if you can't love your brother, whom you can see. Take off the mask.

"The Family Connection"

1 John 4:21 – *"And this commandment have we from him, That he who loveth God love his brother also."*

The diversity of membership in a church always amazes me. Think for a moment about all of the different types of personalities that attend your church. Isn't it hard to comprehend how a group of people that are so different can become family? Most people in the congregation are not blood relatives, nor have they spent most of their lives together. Within the congregation, you have people who have different pay scales, different talents, and are of different mindsets altogether. I suppose the big question that should be asked is, "What is the connection?"

Let me begin by saying it's not just any kind of connection; it is a family connection. The world would look at the church and say they are not a true family. They never lived in the same house growing up, and they are not of the same family tree. This may be true, but they have a much stronger connection. The love of God dwells within their hearts and brings them together.

Have you ever heard someone stand up in church and say, "I'm closer to the church than I am to my blood relatives?" The reason is that the love of God is the strongest connection in this world. Those who love God love the brethren. It is the common denominator in all of our lives and brings us together. You can meet someone you have never seen before and if they are saved there is an instant family connection. This is also evidence that you are in the family. What a wonderful tie that binds us to each other, and then back to our Heavenly Father. The love of God in His children connects them together. Think about all of the precious people you have come to love and know because you met the Lord. Take the time to thank Him for this family connection.

1 John 5

1 Whosoever believeth that Jesus is the Christ is born of God: and every one that loveth him that begat loveth him also that is begotten of him.

2 By this we know that we love the children of God, when we love God, and keep his commandments.

3 For this is the love of God, that we keep his commandments: and his commandments are not grievous.

4 For whatsoever is born of God overcometh the world: and this is the victory that overcometh the world, even our faith.

5 Who is he that overcometh the world, but he that believeth that Jesus is the Son of God?

6 This is he that came by water and blood, even Jesus Christ; not by water only, but by water and blood. And it is the Spirit that beareth witness, because the Spirit is truth.

7 For there are three that bear record in heaven, the Father, the Word, and the Holy Ghost: and these three are one.

8 And there are three that bear witness in earth, the Spirit, and the water, and the blood: and these three agree in one.

9 If we receive the witness of men, the witness of God is greater: for this is the witness of God which he hath testified of his Son.

10 He that believeth on the Son of God hath the witness in himself: he that believeth not God hath made him a liar; because he believeth not the record that God gave of his Son.

11 And this is the record, that God hath given to us eternal life, and this life is in his Son.

12 He that hath the Son hath life; and he that hath not the Son of God hath not life.

13 These things have I written unto you that believe on the name of the Son of God; that ye may know that ye have eternal life, and that ye may believe on the name of the Son of God.

14 And this is the confidence that we have in him, that, if we ask any thing according to his will, he heareth us:

15 And if we know that he hear us, whatsoever we ask, we know that we have the petitions that we desired of him.

16 If any man see his brother sin a sin which is not unto death, he shall ask, and he shall give him life for them that sin not unto death. There is a sin unto death: I do not say that he shall pray for it.

17 All unrighteousness is sin: and there is a sin not unto death.

18 We know that whosoever is born of God sinneth not; but he that is begotten of God keepeth himself, and that wicked one toucheth him not.

19 And we know that we are of God, and the whole world lieth in wickedness.

20 And we know that the Son of God is come, and hath given us an understanding, that we may know him that is true, and we are in him that is true, even in his Son Jesus Christ. This is the true God, and eternal life.

21 Little children, keep yourselves from idols. Amen.

"Keeping the Right Attitude"

1 John 5:1 – *"Whosoever believeth that Jesus is the Christ is born of God: and every one that loveth him that begat loveth him also that is begotten of him."*

This verse teaches that our attitude toward God has everything to do with our attitude toward man. When believers have a right relationship with God, they have a right relationship with each other. They love each other because they are loving Him. Love toward God and His children is a mark of identification for every born-again believer.

I once knew an individual who was faithful to the church but always complained about the preacher or other members within the church. It did not matter how well the church was doing, this person would always complain and find something to be unhappy about. It was clear that this person was miserable and did a good job making everyone else miserable.

Then one day, the unexpected happened. This individual went to the House of God, and the preacher preached a fiery sermon on hell. He fell under deep Holy Ghost conviction, saw himself as a sinner, and got gloriously saved. When he got saved, an amazing thing happened. He stopped complaining about the preacher, the people, and all that was happening at the church. He got involved in all of the events and was kind to everyone. He not only stopped complaining about the church but started doing the opposite of what he used to do. He began to brag on the pastor and the church as if it were the greatest church in the world. Friend, the church didn't change. The pastor had not changed. The individual is the one who changed. He got born again, and his relationship with God changed his relationship with the brethren. He developed the right attitude without because he had the right attitude within.

"Do I Really Love God?"

1 John 5:2 – *"By this we know that we love the children of God, when we love God, and keep his commandments."*

I remember hearing a preacher tell the story about when he was younger, riding down the road with a much older and wiser man of God. After some time on the road, he sensed an awkward silence in the vehicle. The older preacher was a man of few words. Being young and wanting to make a good impression on the older man, he thought he would strike up a spiritual conversation to break the silence.

He spoke out and said to the old preacher, "Brother, I sure do love Jesus, don't you?" The older preacher never smiled and never looked over, but replied by saying, "I'm not really sure if I do or not." This startled the young man. This great man of God had preached all over and had been faithful to the cause of Christ. He sat there in awkward silence, thinking about what he should say now because it was not the answer that he had expected.

After a few moments, he had convinced himself that the man of God had not heard him clearly, so he spoke up again, this time with even more enthusiasm. He said, "Brother, I sure do love Jesus, and I know you love Him too!" The old preacher replied again and said, "As I told you a while ago, I'm not sure if I love Him or not." This shook the young man even more. This was his hero in the faith. How could he say such a thing?

Finally, he said to the old preacher, "Brother, I don't understand how you could say that you are not sure if you love Jesus or not when you have proclaimed Him to others all these years."

The old preacher replied, "Because Jesus said, 'If you love me, keep my commandments,' and I don't always do that." The young man realized that loving Christ was more than just saying it. Loving Him is showing it. We not only show it toward Him but toward others. A Spirit-filled saint will love both God and His children.

"Removing the Grief"

1 John 5:3 – *"For this is the love of God, that we keep his commandments: and his commandments are not grievous."*

John's message throughout this Epistle has been dominated by love. Love is the evidence of life. A dead man knows nothing, sees nothing, hears nothing, and feels nothing. When we were lost, we were dead in our trespasses and sins. Because there was no life of God in us, there was no love of God in us.

This verse reveals the divinity of love, the deeds of love, and the delight of love. God's love is seen in the life of believers when they joyfully keep His commandments. This means they keep His commandments with a smile and not a frown. They don't see obedience as bondage but as an honor. Have you ever seen an obedient saint who was miserable? I understand that someone who is miserably trying to obey God is not one hundred percent obedient. However, the point I'm trying to make is that something is wrong when keeping His commandments produces grief in our lives.

This means that our relationship is not what it should be. Something has stolen our love for serving Him. When we love someone, obeying or serving them is an opportunity to make them happy. That is what we desire when we love them. Too many believers today are miserable because they are more interested in making themselves happy, rather than making the Lord happy.

Keeping the commandments of a loved one is not only an opportunity to serve, but it becomes an obsession. A wife spends her life serving, pleasing, and caring for her husband, not with grief but with joy. Why? She does this because of love. Children who love their parents desire to obey their commandments because they love them. Love will always remove the grief in obedience. Do you find it grievous to obey His commandments?

"How To Have Victory Over the World"

1 John 5:4 – *"For whatsoever is born of God overcometh the world: and this is the victory that overcometh the world, even our faith."*

We cannot defeat the world and its system within ourselves. No matter who we are or how strong we think we may be, man has proven that he is no match for the world he lives in. Education, reformation, morality, religion, riches, power, and prestige have all failed. The world is simply too powerful for man. The pull of the world and the pride of life will swallow him whole every time, leaving him lifeless and empty in the end.

However, there is an answer to this problem. Man does not have to live defeated; he can have victory over this world. This victory comes through being born again. Faith in Christ Jesus leads to the new birth. The new birth promises us victory. This means we are no longer a slave to the world and its system. We can overcome the world through faith in Christ.

If you know you are saved, then realize that God has given you the victory needed to conquer the world every day. Our victory comes from within, not from without. The Holy Spirit within us gives us victory over the world. He teaches us to follow His Word and to do His will. Walking by faith and trusting the Spirit's control allows us to gain victory over the world.

Simply exercise faith in His Word and His will for your life. Learn to walk in His ways by carefully studying the Bible. Allow it to be your instruction manual for life. Seek His will and have faith that His path leads to victory. Remember, we do not have to be in bondage to the world. God wants us to have victory over the world. We can be overcomers through Christ Jesus.

"No Doubt About It!"

1 John 5:5 – *"Who is he that overcometh the world, but he that believeth that Jesus is the Son of God?"*

There are those who ask if Jesus was even real. Did He really exist? Is He nothing more than a myth? While history proves that Jesus lived upon this earth, some still choose not to believe in His existence. They would rather deny the facts and live in ignorance than face this reality. They fear that if His existence is true, then everything else about Jesus could be true. These truths are more than some unbelievers want to deal with, so they just deny Him altogether.

Then, some say He did exist, but He was just a man. They believe He was nothing more than someone who went about doing good and caring for those who were in need. They believe historically He existed but have no faith in His Spirituality.

Others teach that Jesus not only existed historically but that He was a prophet. He was a teacher who was able to perform miracles in the name of the Lord. They place Him on the same level as Moses or Elijah. They teach that He was the son of Mary, but He was not the "Only begotten Son of God." Their denial is just as damnable as the rest.

The Bible clearly declares Him to be the "Only begotten Son of God." He is God in the flesh and the Savior of all men. This is a truth that cannot be denied. Our verse makes this clear, as well as many passages throughout the Scriptures. From the Book of Genesis to the end of Revelation, we can see Christ as who He is. I'm thankful that in a world filled with doubt, there can be no doubt about it! Jesus is the Son of God!

"The Spirit Is Truth"

1 John 5:6 – *"This is he that came by water and blood, even Jesus Christ; not by water only, but by water and blood. And it is the Spirit that beareth witness, because the Spirit is truth."*

When Jesus was baptized, the Father spoke out of heaven saying He was well pleased. The Spirit descended from heaven in the form of a dove upon Jesus at His baptism, as confirmation of what the Father had spoken. The Creator's stamp of approval was both heard and seen that day. This is what John means when he says He came by water. He testified of the life Jesus had lived from His birth to His baptism.

Our verse also declares that He did not come just by water but also by blood. The Spirit of God was instrumental at the birth of the Savior, as well as at His baptism. Jesus was born of a virgin womb. He was conceived of the Holy Ghost. This means that the blood flowing through Christ's veins was not the blood of man, but of God! The Spirit moved on the writers of the New Testament to declare this throughout the Scriptures. We know that His blood is Holy blood because the Bible tells us this truth.

The Spirit bears witness by water and blood that Jesus Christ is the Son of God. What a blessed assurance! If you have the Spirit living inside of you, there is a connection and confirmation with what this verse states. You know it to be true because the Spirit of truth inside of you confirms it. He will bear witness of Jesus and not Himself. We must follow His leadership and do the same. Every believer has the responsibility to bear witness of the sinless life Jesus lived and the sacrificial life He laid down. What a blessing to know that our witness is true! We do not serve a false God, a dead Jesus, or a corrupt Spirit. Our God is true; Jesus is alive, and the Spirit of God is Holy! Take the time to bear witness to someone today.

"The Unity of the Trinity"

1 John 5:7 – *"For there are three that bear record in heaven, the Father, the Word, and the Holy Ghost: and these three are one."*

What a blessing to know that there is unity in the Trinity! When Christ was baptized, all three individuals of the Godhead emerged. God the Father spoke out of heaven, God the Son came out of the water, and God the Spirit descended as a dove.

Even though the Father, the Son, and the Holy Spirit are three separate individuals, they are still one, working together without any division. To try and explain this in complete detail would be impossible. A wise preacher once said that "To understand and explain all that there is to know about the Trinity, you would have to be in it." I would say this is a wise assessment. The best way to describe the unity of the Trinity is to look at ourselves. Man is a triune being, created in the image of God Almighty. Allow me to give you an example of what I'm talking about.

Let's pretend you get a phone call and receive a message that a loved one has just passed away. Three things begin to happen at that very moment. Your spirit begins to grieve, your mind begins preparing for the arrangements that need to be made, and then your body goes into motion, carrying out those plans. All three were working separately, yet they were together. One did not try to carry out the other's responsibilities, but when it came time to get in the car and go, they all went together. All three were present at the funeral, and all can give a unified account of what happened because they are one. This is the unity of the Trinity. When the body is right, man has a healthy relationship with God. When the spirit is right, man has a happy relationship with God. When the soul is right, man has a holy relationship with God. The unity of the Trinity always leads us to victory.

"The Witness Stand of Your Life"

1 John 5:8 – "And there are three that bear witness in earth, the Spirit, and the water, and the blood: and these three agree in one."

I want to call to the witness stand of life three earthly witnesses. These witnesses are found in the verse before us. They are the Spirit, the water, and the blood. They witnessed in the life of Jesus while He was on this earth, and they witness in the life of every believer as well. The Spirit was at His baptism and led Him into the wilderness. The water proved both the birth and the baptism of Christ. He was testified to be both God and man. The blood of Calvary testifies Him to be the Lamb of God, which takes away the sin of the world. Just as they agreed in His life, they also testify in agreement to the life of every believer. Let's notice these three faithful witnesses.

The first witness is the Spirit in you. If you are truly born again, then you have the Spirit living on the inside of you. He can testify that you belong to God, for He lives within your heart. If the Spirit were to take the witness stand of your life today, what would He say on your behalf?

The second witness is the water by you. This has to do with your public baptism. Your profession of faith by water baptism will do two things. First, it pleases the Father, for it is an act of obedience. Second, it identifies you as a true believer. It takes the witness stand to tell the world that you are born again.

The third witness is the blood for you. The blood of Jesus on the mercy seat in heaven testifies of our redemption on earth. If the blood has been applied, then you have the blessed assurance of heaven. If the blood has not been applied, then there is no title, deed, or trophy on earth that will get you inside heaven's gate. The blood testifies that we have been born again. While baptism cannot save, it does testify that by our own will we have trusted Christ. The Spirit testifies of salvation that is real in knowing Jesus! How about you today? Do these witnesses agree with you?

"The Witness of God Is Greater"

1 John 5:9 – *"If we receive the witness of men, the witness of God is greater: for this is the witness of God which he hath testified of his Son."*

Why is it so easy for us to believe man and so difficult for us to believe God? Do you ever find yourself in this condition? We have so much faith in some people that we rarely second-guess what they say. People will often say about others they have confidence in, "If he tells you something, you can believe it." They might even say something like, "I know if she says it, then it's the truth." They say it with such faith and assurance as if there can be no doubt. They base it all on the character of the person, and the confidence they have in the individual they are speaking about.

Sometimes, they have this confidence because of how well they know an individual. Maybe they are speaking about a parent, a spouse, or a lifelong friend that they have spent most of their lives around, and they know their behavior and testimony on a more intimate level. This produces such faith in the witness of the individual. They believe them so much that you and I would be wasting our time trying to convince them otherwise.

Every man has proven untrue at some point, and every man has been wrong on many occasions during his lifetime. No individual possesses full knowledge or ability at all times. The potential of a false witness is a possibility with every man. We are all capable of errors, and we have all made our share of them.

However, the witness of God is greater! What God declares can only be true. The Word of God is without error and can never be wrong. We should receive the witness of God over the witness of men. The Bible is our source of strength and stability. I'm thankful for the witness of faithful men, but I'm glad I have a greater witness. The witness of God is far greater and cannot fail. Lord, help me to never doubt you, and to fully trust in Your Word. If God says it, then that settles it!

"The Key That Unlocks the Door"

1 John 5:10 – *"He that believeth on the Son of God hath the witness in himself: he that believeth not God hath made him a liar; because he believeth not the record that God gave of his Son."*

The keyword in this verse is the word "believeth." John mentions it three times in our text. We know that Christ is the only door to heaven. He declared this truth Himself in the Gospel of John. For someone to get to heaven, they must go through the Door. They must go through the Lord Jesus Christ. All are welcome to go through this Door and enter in. The key that opens this Door is faith. That is why John places so much emphasis on the word "believeth."

Imagine with me that a man is standing on the outside of a luxurious palace. He has a key in his hand. The realtor tells him that everything he has ever wanted and everything he will ever need is on the other side of that door. He puts a document in his hand with his name on it, stating that if he will just use the key to unlock the door and go in, he can have it all. The realtor tells him that the one who owns it all and is willing to give it all to him is waiting for him on the other side of that door. All he has to do is use the key that he was given, go in, and claim the promise.

The man now has the record in one hand, the key in the other hand, and a witness who will testify for him. All he has to do is use the key that unlocks the door. Sadly, the man walks away in unbelief. He fails to trust what's been recorded. He fails to trust the one on the other side of the door. He fails to use the key that was placed in his hand. God has given every man a measure of faith. He must choose for himself whether or not he's going to use it. He must decide if he is going to accept Christ by faith.

"For the Record"

1 John 5:11 – *"And this is the record, that God hath given to us eternal life, and this life is in his Son."*

This verse is another one of my favorite verses in this Epistle. There are several reasons why I love this verse, and I want to share them with you in our devotional today. I believe you will agree with me, and I trust they will help you as much as they have helped me.

The first reason is at the beginning of this verse. It begins with John declaring that there is a record. This means that you and I have something we can depend upon because it has been written down. It has been recorded. When something is recorded, it stands as evidence of what has been said or done.

The second reason is because of the subject of this verse. The subject is eternal life. God has made a record concerning eternal life. I'm so thankful that eternal life is not based upon what man has said or written down. Eternal life is based upon what God has said and written down.

The third reason is because of the Son in this verse. The Son is the source of eternal life. Eternal life is in Jesus Christ, and Him alone. If you have trusted Jesus Christ as your Savior, then you have eternal life. Your name has been recorded in heaven. God has a record of your birth.

The fourth reason is because of the sharing of this verse. This verse teaches us that God hath given us eternal life. He has given us what we do not deserve. He has given us eternal life through His Son, Jesus Christ. This verse teaches us very simply the truth of eternal salvation through Christ. The good news is that we can share it with others. We can tell them of God's promise of eternal life if they will believe and accept it. What a joy to know that your salvation is recorded and promised by the One who keeps the record!

"Where Do You Stand?"

1 John 5:12 – *"He that hath the Son hath life; and he that hath not the Son of God hath not life."*

When I read this verse, three things come to my mind. Those thoughts are: what a person, what a possession, and what a problem. These stand out quite vividly to me. Let's look at them for our devotional thought today.

First, notice what a wonderful person is in this verse. John is still talking about Jesus, the Son of God! To possess Him, you must believe that He is the only begotten Son of God. It amazes me that someone as sinful as you and me could be partakers with the Son of God.

Secondly, I see what a possession we have. If you are saved you not only have Jesus, but you have life. This is not talking about physical life, but eternal life! To know that we are going to live forever with Christ is a blessed thought. What a treasure to know that you have the Son of God and the life of God.

The third and final thing I see in this verse is a problem. Those who do not have the Son do not have eternal life. They have no hope in this life nor in the life to come. We who are saved should be telling others about the Son so they can receive this life.

The world still needs the Gospel today. Believers have been commissioned by God to share the Gospel with sinners. We must live our lives in a way that shows Christ and exhibits the life of Jesus. A lost world is dead in their sins and will remain that way if we do not tell them. There is a double blessing in this verse. First, the blessing of knowing that you have eternal life. Second, the blessing of going to those who do not have it and telling them about Jesus. Purpose in your heart today that you are going to enjoy both the blessing of knowing and the blessing of going.

"The Value of a Check"

1 John 5:13 – *"These things have I written unto you that believe on the name of the Son of God; that ye may know that ye have eternal life, and that ye may believe on the name of the Son of God."*

John is going to bring this Epistle to a close very soon. He emphasizes in our verse that he has written to believers "these things" so that they will know that they have eternal life. His purpose is clear, and the content of his Epistle has been just as convincing. The things he has given will help any new convert or struggling believer find the assurance of salvation. He has been inspired by the Holy Spirit to pen down the Word of God.

I like to think, in this verse, that God hands every believer a check. On the check, there is no dollar amount, but something far greater than money. He has given every believer eternal life. We who are saved possess this life now, but one day each of us will cash in on it as we leave this world. We will live eternally like never before. We will live free from sin and sorrow. We will live free from the cares of this world and the tempter who fights against us. In eternity, we will live free from a body of corruption. What a blessing to know you have eternal life!

Whenever I think about this gift, I'm reminded that a check is only as good as the person who signs it. I could write someone a check for a million dollars, but it wouldn't be worth the paper it's written on. I don't have the resources to back it up. If President Trump were to write someone a check for a million dollars, you could take it to the bank and cash it. His signature is what gives the check value. The day the Lord saved you, He gave you eternal life and you can take it to the bank. His signature is what makes it valuable. It is written in the blood of His precious Son who died at Calvary. He has given us the Bible, and the Bible gives us the assurance that the check is good!

"Assurance Brings Confidence"

1 John 5:14 – *"And this is the confidence that we have in him, that, if we ask any thing according to his will, he heareth us:"*

Learning to pray is a blessing, but learning to pray with confidence is an even greater blessing. Every believer faces battles in prayer. If we are not careful, we will get discouraged in our praying and lose confidence. This causes us either to abandon the prayer closet altogether or pray defeated prayers that never amount to anything.

God not only wants us to pray, but He wants us to pray with confidence. He is not talking about confidence within ourselves. This confidence comes from the assurance that we belong to Him. The assurance of our salvation will give us the confidence we need to come before Him and pray. He wants us to know that we are His children and that He wants us to commune with Him. He desires each of His children to bring their needs before Him. This assurance builds the confidence that God is listening to us when we pray.

We can have confidence not only because we are saved but because we are praying according to His will. I believe this is the lifelong lesson of prayer. The more we pray, the more we see God use prayer to shape our will to His. When we first begin to pray, we pray for everything that we think we should be praying for and praying about. The longer we pray, we begin to see the Lord teaching us to pray according to His will and not our own. We learn His mind, and His desires and we learn to pray according to the will of God.

Jesus prayed according to God's will. Remember in the garden when He prayed about the cup? He sought God's will, not His own. When we ask for God's will to be done we can have both assurance and confidence that He has heard us. Answered prayer in our lives is great evidence that we are a true child of God.

"The Answer Is on the Way"

1 John 5:15 – *"And if we know that he hear us, whatsoever we ask, we know that we have the petitions that we desired of him."*

I thought about a certain prayer request that was on my heart. It was not something that I desired for myself but for the church that I pastor. I'll be honest, the petition looked impossible. My flesh told me repeatedly that there was no way it would be granted.

Despite my flesh, my Father said to me, "Pray." I sought God about it earnestly, asking Him to answer the prayer. Instead of looking like God was going to answer, it looked more like it would never happen. What kept me asking Him was that I could clearly see that it was the will of God. I knew, despite my flesh, and despite how impossible it looked, that God promised in His Word that He would grant it. For four years, I prayed and asked the Lord to do this certain thing.

Finally, one morning in prayer, I felt the urgency not only to pray about it but to ask God to answer it in a specific timeline. I began praying that He would answer it by the end of the year. I said, "Lord, if You choose not to answer this request, I'll keep asking until Your will has been accomplished. But I'm asking You to do it by the end of the year." I don't know how to explain this, and I don't know if you will believe it, but I spoke to my wife at Thanksgiving and told her that one of the things I was most thankful for was that God was going to answer this prayer by the end of the year. I'm glad to testify that on the last Sunday of the year, God answered that prayer! The answer was on the way four years ago. He just wanted me to learn that I can trust Him. I'm glad we can know that our prayer has been heard and the answer is on the way.

"A Deadly Path"

1 John 5:16 – *"If any man see his brother sin a sin which is not unto death, he shall ask, and he shall give him life for them that sin not unto death. There is a sin unto death: I do not say that he shall pray for it."*

Three people in the Bible come to mind whenever I think about sinning a sin unto death. Moses was the meekest man in all the earth, but his patience ran thin, and he allowed the bad behavior of others to affect him. His disobedience to God cost him the promised land, and he was not allowed to enter. Moses was the great patriarch of the Old Testament, and this teaches us to be careful because at any point in life, we can venture down this deadly path.

A second person who comes to mind is Achan. He stole the Babylonian garments, the silver, and the wedge of gold. His sin not only led him down this deadly path, but his entire family was taken down with him. We must be careful because sinful living affects those around us. His family paid for his wickedness. What a tragedy, but what a truth we should remember.

Finally, I think about the couple in Acts chapter five, who thought they were deceiving Peter when in reality they were lying to the Holy Ghost. They both died that day as a result of their sinful deceit. This proves that God will tell a preacher when folks are not living right. But even if you do manage to fool the preacher, you cannot fool God. Sin always brings consequences, and sometimes those consequences lead to death.

We never really know the weight of our decisions until it is too late to change them. Then we have to live with the decisions we have made, or perhaps we cannot live because of the decisions we have made. We should always fear sin and never treat it lightly. It could take us down a deadly path at any moment.

"Is It Sin or Not?"

1 John 5:17 – *"All unrighteousness is sin: and there is a sin not unto death."*

The question is often asked, "Does the Bible say this is wrong?" Or you might have heard this one, "Where in the Bible does it say that this is sin?" Usually, these questions are attached to hard subjects with little reference to them, if any at all. They are gray areas that most people would rather avoid than try to answer. Others feel that if they cannot find a chapter and verse that spells it out in black and white, they can automatically assume that God is okay with the subject or situation. After all, had He been concerned with it, He would have written it out plainly for us to read.

The problem with this mentality is that they fail to realize that the Bible is a book of both precepts and principles. Sometimes the Lord spells it out in black and white: "Thou shalt not commit adultery." And other times, He gives us a principle to apply and live by. If a believer has the Word of God in their head and the Holy Spirit in their heart, they can discern what is sin and what is not.

According to James 4:17, sin is failure to do what you know is good. Here in our verse, sin is anything that is unrighteous. These two verses together give us our answer when someone asks the question, "Is this sin or not?" The answer is, "Is it good in the eyes of God, and is it righteous?" If you are saved, and know to do good, and desire to live righteously, then put it under the microscope and see for yourself. Here is an example: Is gambling good within itself? Would it be considered righteous or unrighteous? Ask the same question concerning soul-winning.

I think you will see that you will get two different answers to the questions. When asking the question about whether something is a sin or not depends on your motive. The motive of a believer is not to see how close we can get to sin, but how righteous we can live.

The fact that we have to ask should cause us to completely avoid the subject or situation.

"We Belong to Him"

1 John 5:18 – *"We know that whosoever is born of God sinneth not; but he that is begotten of God keepeth himself, and that wicked one toucheth him not."*

I see two facts in this verse that prove that a believer belongs to Christ. What a blessing to be able to read the Bible and find the blessed assurance that we have been born again. This gives us great comfort and victory over the wicked one mentioned here in our text.

The first fact is that a true child of God cannot continue on a course of sin without receiving chastisement. The word "sinneth" refers to a continuous course of sin. In other words, there is a sin unto death as the previous verses taught us. This draws concern for a lot of people who claim to know Christ but live a continual life of sin with no chastisement. Whenever a believer lives in sin, they are miserable, defeated, and chastised. If they continue to rebel against God, then they run the risk of being taken home early. These are all clear indicators of who they belong to. We know that believers can sin, but a good example would be that of a sheep. A sheep may fall into a mud puddle and get filthy. A sheep might even deliberately go into the mud. But a sheep will not enjoy the mud or wallow in it like a pig because it is not its nature.

The second fact that we belong to Him is that the wicked one cannot touch us. We certainly battle Satan in this life, but God is the one in control of our lives, not Satan. Like Job of old, God puts a hedge around His children and protects us. The devil cannot do anything to us without God's permission, and even then, he is restricted as to what he can do. God has already considered us before the devil has, and knows what we can and cannot take. The Devil has to keep his distance because we belong to Christ!

"A Wicked World"

1 John 5:19 – *"And we know that we are of God, and the whole world lieth in wickedness."*

When you read this verse notice that there are two separate truths placed before us. The first truth is about the saved, and the second truth is about the sinner. We are reminded of the great difference between the child of God and the world that we live in. While we may be in this world, we are not of this world. As the songwriter has said, "This world is not my home."

God's children live in complete assurance of their identity while living in this wicked world. What a great blessing that is as we journey down here. The question in my mind is, why is this world so wicked? *"Why do the heathen rage, and the people imagine a vain thing?"* (Ps. 2:1). The answer is because they do not know God. When someone does not know the way of righteousness, then the only path for them to choose is a path of wickedness. They are destined to follow this path because they are not of God. Some will go further down this road of destruction than others, but they are all on the same path. They are in a world that the Bible says lieth in wickedness.

The way of this world was set a long time ago in Eden's garden and will continue until the King comes and lifts the curse from it. He will rule this world, conquer the kings and captains of this world, and bind and destroy the god of this world, proving that He is the Creator, Conqueror, and King eternal. This is the promise we read about in the Word of God. Until then, God's children are despised and rejected by a world filled with wickedness; but we too can conquer this wicked world because we are of God!

"Wrapping It Up"

1 John 5:20 – *"And we know that the Son of God is come, and hath given us an understanding, that we may know him that is true, and we are in him that is true, even in his Son Jesus Christ. This is the true God, and eternal life."*

Our verse contains two great finds and two great facts. First, there are two great finds. We who are saved have found the Son of God, and through Him, we have found spiritual understanding. These are riches that money cannot buy! To be saved and have understanding removes all fear and gives us hope in this world and the world to come. We understand that we know Christ and that we are in Him. The songwriter said, "I am His, and He is mine forever."

Second, there are two great facts. The first has to do with the reality of the Son and the second has to do with the reality of God. John brings them both together in His final words to remind us that Jesus is the Son of God and that Jesus is God. As we have already stated before, you cannot dissect the Trinity. You cannot believe in God the Father and reject God the Son. They are coequal, and they are coexistent.

Salvation through the Son of God gives us an understanding of the deity of Christ. Just because we may not be able to comprehend or explain it all, does not mean that we do not believe it all. You might say, "Well, preacher, how can you believe in something that you cannot fully comprehend or fully explain?" I can answer that question in one word. It is the word "faith." Faith gives the child of God both confidence and understanding beyond this world's theology.

Will you place your faith in the Lord Jesus Christ as the Son of God? Will you believe that Jesus is the only begotten Son of God? Will you believe Jesus is God? My answer is "yes" to all of these questions. My friend, how about you?

"A Final Word"

1 John 5:21 – *"Little children, keep yourselves from idols. Amen."*

John is closing this great Epistle with a final word of warning. He reminds us to keep ourselves from idols. This may seem like a warning that would not be relevant for us today. I am sure that most readers would say that they do not have wooden statues or graven images hanging on their walls or sitting on the mantle in their living room. Most of us would agree that we do not bow down to an image each morning or pray to idols of any kind. Although I realize many still worship the false idols of wood and stone as they did in days of old, here in America, we have managed to modernize idols.

First, think about the definition of an idol. An idol is anything we allow to come between us and God, anything we place our confidence in more than God, or anything we hold in higher regard than God. People may not make this terrible statement with their lips, but it will be evident in their lives.

For many, sports have become an idol. I remember years ago attending a college football game. While I was sitting in the arena waiting for the team to run out on the field, the music started playing, and I watched as they pulled a cart of huge stone graven mascots to the fifty-yard line. The crowd went wild, and folks started chanting the name of the team. As I watched this, I was grieved and said, "This is idolatry on full display."

There are many other examples of modern-day idols we could talk about. Some have made an idol out of their car, their house, their job, etc. The truth is, we can make anything an idol. Even a good thing can become an idol when we allow it to take over our hearts. Why is it that some are so devoted, so passionate, and so committed to something like the sporting event that I mentioned, but not that way toward God? Friend, keep yourself from the modern idols of this world.

2 John

1 The elder unto the elect lady and her children, whom I love in the truth; and not I only, but also all they that have known the truth;

2 For the truth's sake, which dwelleth in us, and shall be with us for ever.

3 Grace be with you, mercy, and peace, from God the Father, and from the Lord Jesus Christ, the Son of the Father, in truth and love.

4 I rejoiced greatly that I found of thy children walking in truth, as we have received a commandment from the Father.

5 And now I beseech thee, lady, not as though I wrote a new commandment unto thee, but that which we had from the beginning, that we love one another.

6 And this is love, that we walk after his commandments. This is the commandment, That, as ye have heard from the beginning, ye should walk in it.

7 For many deceivers are entered into the world, who confess not that Jesus Christ is come in the flesh. This is a deceiver and an antichrist.

8 Look to yourselves, that we lose not those things which we have wrought, but that we receive a full reward.

9 Whosoever transgresseth, and abideth not in the doctrine of Christ, hath not God. He that abideth in the doctrine of Christ, he hath both the Father and the Son.

10 If there come any unto you, and bring not this doctrine, receive him not into your house, neither bid him God speed:

11 For he that biddeth him God speed is partaker of his evil deeds.

12 Having many things to write unto you, I would not write with paper and ink: but I trust to come unto you, and speak face to face, that our joy may be full.

13 The children of thy elect sister greet thee. Amen.

"A Mysterious Lady"

2 John 1 – *"The elder unto the elect lady and her children, whom I love in the truth; and not I only, but also all they that have known the truth;"*

The lady that John refers to in our text is a mysterious lady. Her identity seems to be concealed in the text and has been greatly debated among Bible students. Who is she? Why did John not call her name? These are only a few of the questions surrounding her. Let us consider this mysterious lady and who she could be.

Some believe that she is the church. They believe John was writing to the church and addressed her as the "elect lady." They believe that "her children" could be the saints fellowshipping in the church, and the "elect sister," in verse thirteen, to be a sister church. One thing to consider is that the church is never referred to as a "lady," or a "woman," but as a "chaste virgin." These are titles given to the nation of Israel.

Another thought is that she is Mary, the mother of Jesus. It is possible that Mary could still be alive, but she would be a very elderly woman. It would make sense for John to refer to her as the "elect lady." His motive could be to hide her identity because it would put her in great danger due to the persecution of Christians in his day.

Another interesting teaching is that she is a godly, respectable lady whom John knew. He was writing to encourage her, her children, and her sister in the faith. John wanted to give her instructions and strength for the journey.

Whoever she is, we see that John and everyone who knew her loved her, according to verse one. She had a great impact on this old soldier of the cross. She was a tremendous blessing to him in the truth. This lady is both mysterious and wondrous in her hidden identity. It is proof that you do not have to be well-known to have influence or to be a blessing. God knows who she is!

"Forever True"

2 John 2 – *"For the truth's sake, which dwelleth in us, and shall be with us for ever."*

John is emphasizing the truth in the early verses of this Epistle. He wants to warn this elect lady and her children concerning the lies of false teachers. In verse one, he speaks about the love for the truth and the knowledge of the truth. Then in verse two, he speaks about the triumph of the truth. The truth will last forever! What a blessing to know that every lie will one day be washed away by God's eternal truth!

If we look closely, there is an even greater blessing in verse two. The Bible declares that this truth dwells within the believer. Whenever an individual is saved, God's Spirit takes His abode in their heart. The Spirit of Truth connects us with the Word of Truth. The Holy Spirit reveals to us the truths of God's Word and gives us understanding. He enlightens us and places these truths within us.

Truth within us gives us victory, peace, and joy. These are qualities that the world does not possess because the world does not know the truth. The Bible is our guide and stability in this world. We have blessed assurance because of what God said, not because of how we feel. Our belief is built upon facts and not feelings. Feelings will come and go, but as stated in our text, truth shall be with us forever.

The more truth an individual knows the freer he will live. Make it your goal in life to be a student of the Word of God. Build your life around the truth and stand upon its principles and teachings. Take the time to share the truth with those who may have never heard the Word of God. Always take the time to thank God that you had the privilege of knowing, hearing, and receiving the truth.

"Three Precious Friends"

2 John 3 – *"Grace be with you, mercy, and peace, from God the Father, and from the Lord Jesus Christ, the Son of the Father, in truth and love."*

Our verse opens with what I like to call three precious friends. I want to introduce them to you. The first is Mr. Grace, the second is Mr. Mercy, and the third is Mr. Peace. If you are saved, then you can testify that you know each of them quite well. They have been sent to you from God the Father and His Son, the Lord Jesus Christ, in all truth and love. Everything I just said is contained in this one verse. What a blessing to enjoy the help of these individuals along our journey through life.

Mr. Grace is present at the birth of a child of God and is fully committed to helping him cross the river into the Celestial City. He will be there in his time of need, to give him strength whenever it is needed. Mr. Grace blesses God's children on their journey, to remind them how much the Father loves and cares for them. He is a true friend to the believer each day that he lives.

Mr. Mercy has been in the believer's life longer than he would ever be able to acknowledge. He has walked beside him as both a sinner and a saint. Before his conversion, when he should have been in hell, Mr. Mercy kept him from getting what he deserved. During all of his times of foolishness and unbelief, he was held in the arms of Mr. Mercy, when Mr. Wrath was ready to come in to proclaim rightful justice. Mr. Mercy still follows along to help God's child find forgiveness whenever it is needed.

Mr. Peace is a friend who gives calmness and stability, even when God's child has no answer or understanding. He whispers to the traveler, "everything is going to be all right," even when his world is falling apart. He stays with him and smothers him with his presence at the crossing from this life into the next.

These are three precious friends who will be with us until we see the Father and the Son face to face.

"Stay on the Path"

2 John 4 – "I rejoiced greatly that I found of thy children walking in truth, as we have received a commandment from the Father."

John is excited to hear of these believers walking in the truth. He reminds them that it has been commanded by the Father. He encourages them by letting them know how they have encouraged him by simply staying on this path. He is going to deal with the danger of unscriptural ways in this Epistle, so he begins by acknowledging their dedication to staying with what is right.

We live in a day that is a lot like the day John was facing when it comes to truth and error. There are many false teachers and false teachings in our present world today. Whenever we see others remaining faithful and abiding by the Book, it lifts our spirits. I want to encourage you, dear reader, not to dip your colors in these last days. Do not deviate or change course in these final steps of the Christian race. Keep walking the path you have been on. If it was right back then, it is still right now.

When a brother or sister stops walking in truth, it is heartbreaking. We all know people, more than we care to remember, who have turned back. Make up your mind, if you have not already, that by the grace of God, you will not be a casualty in the work of God. Say to yourself, "that if none go with me, still I'm going to follow Jesus all the days of my life." Stay on this path and keep walking in the truth of God's Word!

One day, we will come to the end of the pathway, and our Savior will be standing at the end of it. Our desire should be to hear Him say, "Well done, My child," as we take those final steps. Remember, this is the greatest pathway we could ever take! How blessed we are to tread the pathway of God. Avoid all detours and stay on the path!

"Nothing New to Say"

2 John 5 – *"And now I beseech thee, lady, not as though I wrote a new commandment unto thee, but that which we had from the beginning, that we love one another."*

John reminds this dear lady that his letter contains nothing new, but it is a reminder of what she has heard from the beginning. What makes the Bible so unique is that it is an old message that is up to date for any generation, any time, and anywhere. The message is relevant, clear, and steady. The commandments of this Book never change.

John reminds her of the commandment our Savior gave to "love one another." Love is the passion and the principle for the Christian life. When John speaks about love, he is speaking about Christ's love. A love that knows no boundaries or limitations. This is an amazing love that prevails over all sin and conquers all of the evils that can poison a man's heart.

The love of Christ is to be exhibited in the life of every believer and is to be the tie that binds all of His children together. His love is the common denominator in all of our lives. Each of us can look around and testify that if we had not known the love of God we most likely would not have known each other. His love has connected us as believers. One day we will experience this love at its fullest. We will see Jesus face to face and be standing in the love of our Father in a glorified body. We will be in an environment with no hatred, envy, or strife, and all will be perfect and complete. We will have full knowledge and understanding, and we will be able to enjoy the glories of heaven and the love of God as never before. It is at that moment that we will love one another in perfect union and harmony. Until then, we are to endeavor to love one another as the Bible commands.

"Do You Love God?"

2 John 6 – *"And this is love, that we walk after his commandments. This is the commandment, That, as ye have heard from the beginning, ye should walk in it."*

I am sure that if you walked up to the average church member today and asked them if they loved God, they would quickly respond by saying, "Yes." They might even look at you with astonishment that you would dare question their love for God. The fact that they attend church and call themselves a Christian should be evidence enough that they love Him. But the truth is, going to church and saying you love God is not enough evidence to others or God Himself that you truly love Him.

Our verse says that love is seen by walking in His commandments. Jesus said in John 14:15, "If ye love me, keep my commandments." Obedience declares our devotion and commitment to God. It expresses to those we come in contact with that we love Him. Do not misunderstand what I am saying; I believe we should testify that we love Him. However, some say they love Him, but they do not walk in His commandments. This kind of lifestyle places a big question mark on what they declare. If you love Him, then why do you not obey Him? On the other hand, some may not shout it as loud as others do with their lips, but you can look at their lives and there is no doubt that they deeply love God.

People have become accustomed to attending church on Sunday and singing "Oh how I love Jesus," then leaving, going about their lives, doing their own thing, and not living by the commandments of God. It is quite simple; a faithful spouse declares with their life that they love their companion. An unfaithful spouse may say it all day long, but their actions speak louder than their words. Look at your life and ask yourself, "Do I love God?"

"Watch Out for Impostors"

2 John 7 – "For many deceivers are entered into the world, who confess not that Jesus Christ is come in the flesh. This is a deceiver and an antichrist."

John uses the word "deceivers" twice in this verse. It is the Greek word "planos," and it is a word suggesting "impostors." These were men who denied the incarnation of Jesus Christ. John even goes so far as to call them an "antichrist." As deceivers, they became the enemy of men, and as antichrists, they became the enemy of God.

We know that these impostors still exist today. Some false teachers and preachers deny that Jesus is God in the flesh. They reject the fact that Jesus is more than just a man. They refuse to believe that He is the God-man. These impostors are easy for us to spot today and are not a temptation to follow for most readers.

However, there are many impostors today in our ranks that we must be cautious about. We cannot allow the charisma and personality of impostors to persuade us from the truth. There are many who fall prey to heretical teachings because of the way they look or sound. We should view what others say in light of what the Scripture teaches.

Do not make the mistake of thinking you are past the point of being deceived. I once had a dear friend who preached the truth of God's Word with power and authority. He stood in my pulpit and preached sermons that helped our church and greatly influenced my Christian life. I do not believe he was a false prophet or a false teacher. However, he was deceived and no longer believes many of the things he once preached and stood for. What happened? Perhaps he reached the point of thinking he could not be deceived. We must always be clinging to the truth of God's Word. "Buy the truth, and sell it not," is what the Book says. Watch out for impostors!

"Threats and Thieves"

2 John 8 – "Look to yourselves, that we lose not those things which we have wrought, but that we receive a full reward."

We are quickly given the admonition in this verse to keep our eyes open! Do not allow heresy to overtake you. False doctrines and teachers are nothing to take lightly. They are everywhere and should be considered both a threat and a thief. False teachers never produce or build anything. They simply prey on the weak and vulnerable and steal from the fold.

They should be regarded as thieves and avoided like the plague. If you lend them an ear, they may not only deceive you, but their poisonous doctrines could cost you eternal rewards at the judgment seat. I am not indicating the loss of any man's salvation. We understand that salvation is eternal and that no man or devil in hell can cause a believer to lose their salvation.

However, they can prevent you from receiving a full reward at the judgment seat of Christ. False doctrine can get a believer off course and cause them to miss the will of God for their life. I have seen young converts with great promise for the ministry get sidetracked and fall into false doctrine. The end result is that they will never live up to the potential the Lord had intended for them.

Calvinism is on the rise, and there are those in our realm who have flirted with this false doctrine. The fact is, no one becomes a Calvinist from reading the Bible. To believe this false doctrine, you have to read after another Calvinist. This will rob an individual of receiving the soul winner's crown at the judgment seat. This is one example of how false teachers are both a threat and a thief to those who are willing to listen.

"Get Off the Fence"

2 John 9 – "Whosoever transgresseth, and abideth not in the doctrine of Christ, hath not God. He that abideth in the doctrine of Christ, he hath both the Father and the Son."

We must remember that John is older and is coming to the shoreline of life and eternity. He does not have many days left on this earth and has no time for wasting words. He makes his statement both bold and clear. You are either in or out. You are either saved or lost. You either have God, or you don't. He makes no exceptions, and he makes no excuses for the reader in this text. There is no room for sitting on the fence in this verse.

A lot of folks want to sit on the fence today. They are saying one thing but believing or doing another. I am glad the Scripture makes it clear that you either believe the Bible or you don't. You either abide in the truth, or you don't. You either have salvation, or you don't.

We tend to excuse people for departing from the faith. Let's face the cold, hard truth that, while some have been a Demas or a John Mark, most have never experienced true salvation. They walked away because they never really had a relationship with God in the first place. They were actors who got tired of playing the part. They never really believed what they said they did, so they did not abide in the truth.

Evidence that you are a true believer is that you are still believing today. Believers believe and keep on believing. They believe more and more of the truth as they continue to abide in the Word. Truth always comes down to doctrine, and those who don't believe the truth will be carried away by some new doctrine that comes along. When it comes to the truth you are either on one side of the fence or the other. You cannot sit on the fence.

"Do Not Let Them in Your House"

2 John 10 – *"If there come any unto you, and bring not this doctrine, receive him not into your house, neither bid him God speed:"*

There are several things to consider in our verse when it comes to false teachers. For starters, you don't have to worry about finding cults; they will find you. The Bible says they will come to your residence. I think this verse should also shame anyone who does not believe in door-to-door visitation. How sad it is when the average Mormon or Jehovah's "false" Witness will spend over fifteen hours a week knocking on doors to promote their false doctrines, but the average Christian will not pass out a tract or show up for a one-hour visitation on Saturday morning. Even many of our so-called fundamental churches have canceled their door-to-door visitation programs altogether. It is no wonder that cults are on the rise.

John tells us that when they come, do not let them in your house, and do not say goodbye to them when they leave. Do not show hospitality to those who work against the Bible. For some, this may seem a little over the top, but I remind you that it is straight out of the Book. God takes it very offensively and very seriously whenever someone denounces His Word and tries to poison others with their devilish doctrine. We should have the same attitude toward them.

This does not mean we are to be belligerent and rude. The Bible does not instruct us to cause a scene or create a controversy. It simply instructs us not to allow them in our house and not to bid them a good day. These people are dangerous, and the slightest kindness may lead to a misstep with you or someone in your home. Allowing them through the doorway of your home could be the first step to allowing them through the doorway of your heart, so don't let them in at all. Deal with it before it goes any further.

"Hooking Up With the Heathen"

2 John 11 – "For he that biddeth him God speed is partaker of his evil deeds."

Most of us would never see ourselves hooking up with the heathens of this world. We do not worship the same God, nor do we have the same interests in mind. The big question is not how we see it but rather how God sees it. He always sees things more clearly than we do.

In this verse, the Lord draws a narrow line for those who would show a false teacher hospitality. The Bible says if you show him kindness, then you are a partaker of his evil deeds. There is some pretty strong language in this text. Do you mean to tell me that just one kind gesture links me to his entire agenda? Why would the Lord be so harsh in this judgment?

The reason is that it encourages the false teacher to continue. It makes him feel good about what he is doing and blinds him to his error. A false teacher needs to experience rejection and confrontation with the truth. He is not going to receive this from the world, so the responsibility is upon our shoulders. If there is any chance of him seeing the error of his ways, then it will only come by us standing against his teaching and not encouraging him in his evil deeds.

Another reason is that if you show him kindness, then how much further will he go? It is no different than the devil himself showing up at your house, knocking on the door, and wanting to come in. He's not going to show up with horns, a tail, dressed in red with a pitchfork. If he did show up like this, would you tell him to have a good day? The answer is "no" because you want nothing to do with him. God says to have the same attitude toward false teachers. They are the devil showing up with a book in their hand, neatly dressed, and with a friendly smile. They are waiting to see if you will let them in or at least bid them a good day. Say nothing good that links you to their evil deeds.

"I Wonder If He Got to See Her?"

2 John 12 – *"Having many things to write unto you, I would not write with paper and ink: but I trust to come unto you, and speak face to face, that our joy may be full."*

You will have to decide for yourself who you believe the identity of this lady is. Is she Mary, the mother of Jesus? Is she a well-respected lady in the community? Is she the local church? These are questions for you, the reader, to sort out.

However, we do know that John had a strong desire to see her. He has many things to say to her, and the thought of fellowshipping together would have given them both great joy. These are facts that we read about in this verse. There are also things in the verse of great wonder.

One mystery of our text is, what else did John want to say to her? What were the "many things" he desired to write to her? No doubt, it was more spiritual instructions to help her stand in the day in which she was living. The Holy Spirit did not want us to have those instructions, or He would have moved on John to have written them.

Another question is, why did John choose not to write those things down from a human standpoint? We accept that it is God's letter, not John's, but I still cannot help but wonder what went through his mind. Maybe he was too tired to write the "many things." Perhaps he thought it would be better to say them face to face.

The final mystery in this text is, did he ever get to see her? We know that he had the expectation and desire. His age and his health were no doubt factors; time was no longer on his side. Would he be able to get to her to have that final conversation? If not here, no doubt he would over yonder! It does not matter who this lady is, for we know heaven finally brought them together face to face.

"Time Has Made a Change"

2 John 13 – *"The children of thy elect sister greet thee. Amen."*

John has penned his final verse in this small Epistle, and I have to say that he has not disappointed us with his closing remark. This verse is unique because it contains both a farewell and a greeting. John is saying goodbye with his pen, but he extends a greeting through this elect lady's nieces and nephews. Some believe the elect sister and the elect lady are two local churches in the same neighborhood. This may very well be true, but they could also be two literal sisters.

What the text does reveal is that time has made a change in this aged apostle. We now see the tender side of this old "son of thunder" (Mark 3:17). He is getting closer to his final flight and shows the desire to be a blessing and encouragement to all he has contact with.

Doesn't time have a way of doing that with all of God's children? The closer we get to the shores of home, the more sensitive we become to the needs of others around us. There is a level of sensitivity that comes in the final stretch of the race of life that we do not find anywhere else along the journey. We are more aware of the needs of others, as we view every day as it may be our last, and every visitation with others as if it is the final one.

Time has made a change in us slowly but surely. It is preparing us for that final exit. We are trying to encourage and prepare those that we see along the way. John was a blessing both in his words and his witness to this lady and her sister. He had a burden for them all to do well in the work of God. He became both the instructor and the encourager in this Epistle. His heart and his devotion can easily be seen when reading these thirteen verses. This is a great example for us to follow as we walk in truth.

3 John

1 The elder unto the wellbeloved Gaius, whom I love in the truth.

2 Beloved, I wish above all things that thou mayest prosper and be in health, even as thy soul prospereth.

3 For I rejoiced greatly, when the brethren came and testified of the truth that is in thee, even as thou walkest in the truth.

4 I have no greater joy than to hear that my children walk in truth.

5 Beloved, thou doest faithfully whatsoever thou doest to the brethren, and to strangers;

6 Which have borne witness of thy charity before the church: whom if thou bring forward on their journey after a godly sort, thou shalt do well:

7 Because that for his name's sake they went forth, taking nothing of the Gentiles.

8 We therefore ought to receive such, that we might be fellowhelpers to the truth.

9 I wrote unto the church: but Diotrephes, who loveth to have the preeminence among them, receiveth us not.

10 Wherefore, if I come, I will remember his deeds which he doeth, prating against us with malicious words: and not content therewith, neither doth he himself receive the brethren, and forbiddeth them that would, and casteth them out of the church.

11 Beloved, follow not that which is evil, but that which is good. He that doeth good is of God: but he that doeth evil hath not seen God.

12 Demetrius hath good report of all men, and of the truth itself: yea, and we also bear record; and ye know that our record is true.

13 I had many things to write, but I will not with ink and pen write unto thee:

14 But I trust I shall shortly see thee, and we shall speak face to face. Peace be to thee. Our friends salute thee. Greet the friends by name.

"Elderly Encouragement"

3 John 1 – *"The elder unto the wellbeloved Gaius, whom I love in the truth."*

There is no doubt that John is an aged apostle in this brief Epistle. He is in the final stretch of his ministry and is preparing to make his grand exit soon. He uses the word "elder" in this verse, which can describe the apostle both spiritually and physically. He has something to say to a dear Christian brother that will certainly be a great encouragement to him.

I thought about how important it is to have the encouragement of elders. I use the term "elder" just as I see John in our text. God has placed Christian people in all of our lives that fit this profile. You see, John has the years behind him, the yearning within him, and the yonder before him. He could offer this brother a level of encouragement that others might not be able to give. While youth may give a man a wealth of opportunities, years can give a man a wealth of observation. It is with this wealth that he is able to encourage others to keep pressing on in the truth.

The testimony and the tenderness of John are both seen in this verse. As an elder, he had kept a good testimony, proven himself to be qualified, and proven to be faithful through the seasons of life. He now expresses his love for this brother in the truth of God's Word.

Names and faces come to mind when I think of the people God has placed in my life to encourage me in the truth. Take the time today to reflect on those "elders" God has placed in your life to encourage you in the faith. They have loved us, instructed us, and been tremendous examples of how a Christian is supposed to live. Today we pay tribute to "The Elder."

"What Is Your Number One Wish?"

3 John 2 – *"Beloved, I wish above all things that thou mayest prosper and be in health, even as thy soul prospereth."*

In this verse, the apostle uses the phrase, "I wish above all things." This phrase seemed to catch my eye as I read it. I'm interested in what his number one wish would be concerning our brother Gaius. We can see that John wastes no time in revealing what he wished for.

John desired for him to prosper financially and physically, just as he had prospered spiritually. I'm sure the health and wealth, name it and claim it crowd loves this verse. We must remember that there is more connected to this verse than just that alone. Time will not allow us to chase that rabbit, but let me say that the message of the Bible is not material wealth and physical health, but spiritual deliverance from sin, Satan, and self. These are riches that money cannot buy.

There is no doubt that John thought this man would be able to use the financial gain for the work of this ministry. Gaius most likely had poor health, so it was also the apostle's desire to see him experience a physical touch. There is no envy or covetousness in John's soul, but a desire to see the children of God prosper in every way possible. This was his number one wish for his brother. In this self-centered world, there must be a desire in all of our hearts to see others being blessed more than ourselves.

It reminds us that Christian living is not about getting; it is about giving. It's about desiring more for others than we do for ourselves. As John prepares to make his final flight, he desires nothing less than the fullest of God's blessings upon the children of God. Think about another brother today and ask yourself this question, "What is your number one wish for them?"

"What the Brethren Say About You"

3 John 3 – *"For I rejoiced greatly, when the brethren came and testified of the truth that is in thee, even as thou walkest in the truth."*

I heard a preacher say years ago, "You cannot win every battle, everybody, and every brother." I think this is a statement that has proven to be true in my life. Regarding the brethren, some seemingly can never be satisfied. We go crazy trying to please them or meet their standard of approval. When I make these statements, I am not talking about lowering our standards of dress, music, or doctrinal beliefs. That is the route most are headed when they start using this type of terminology. I'm just saying, sometimes you have to divorce yourself from public opinion and live for God.

On the other hand, our verse teaches that we are accountable to the brethren, to a degree. The reason is that our spiritual well-being is at stake. It was the brethren who delivered the report to the apostle concerning the beloved Gaius. Paul rejoices because it was reported that he is still walking in the truth.

In a day when so-called preachers and churches want to act as if there is no moral or doctrinal obligation to each other, we must keep a good testimony. Your testimony among the brethren does matter! The report that circulates about you should not be one of compromise, but that you are still walking in the truth.

Just as the report encourages the apostle in our text, it could have discouraged him to have heard that he had become a casualty. We should feel a responsibility to carry on the principles, doctrines, and standards of those faithful men and women who have taught us and gone on before us. I think of the words of the old song, "May all who come behind us find us faithful." By the grace of God, be consistent in where you walk and stand. What the brethren say about

you should matter because it will either cause people to rejoice or
weep.

"The Soul Winner's Trophy"

3 John 4 – *"I have no greater joy than to hear that my children walk in truth."*

John was responsible for bringing Gaius to Christ. In our verse, he calls him one of his children. It is a tremendous blessing when God uses you to help bring someone to Christ. It is an even greater blessing when you hear that they are growing and walking in the truth of God's Word. John was overjoyed at the testimony of his convert.

We must not forget that as believers we are to both evangelize and equip others in the ministry. Discipleship is an important part of helping others get established in their new life. Once an individual begins to blossom in the faith, it gives strength and encouragement, not just to them but to all of the church. New converts add excitement to the church like no others can do.

As soul winners, we can be encouraged by looking back at some of the trophies of grace God has allowed us to have a part in. We must not pride ourselves, nor fool ourselves, in thinking that we have done anything. The Lord could have done it without us. He could have used someone else to witness and win them. I know there are certain people that only we can reach, but that doesn't mean God is limited. This only means we have a personal responsibility because God placed them in our paths.

I once knew of two great preachers in our area, who are in heaven now. The first was a faithful country preacher, and the second was a lost man who was a local barber. The country preacher kept witnessing and preaching to the man until he was converted. He then became a powerful preacher like the one who had brought him to Christ. I had the privilege of listening to them preach revivals together many times. I often wondered what the older of the two must have thought as he sat and listened to this trophy of grace thunder from the pulpit. He must have greatly rejoiced to hear this child as he walked in the truth.

"Open Doors"

3 John 5 – *"Beloved, thou doest faithfully whatsoever thou doest to the brethren, and to strangers;"*

John is still praising Gaius in our verse, now focusing on his faithfulness to the brethren. This servant had proven to be a faithful help and blessing to the men of God who would pass by. He knew some of these preachers on a personal level, such as the apostle John. Other preachers passing by were strangers to him, but he offered to them the same faithful spirit and service. They discovered two open doors awaiting their arrival when meeting Gaius.

The first was the open door of his heart. Gaius was sincere in his service. He loved the Lord and loved those who labored for Him. He desired nothing in return but wanted to be a blessing to men of God on their journey. Whenever people love the Lord, they look for opportunities to be a blessing. Because their heart is open to the Savior, it is also open to service. Whenever someone's heart is not right, it is very difficult to get them to be faithful in service. Gaius opened the door of his heart.

Second, he opened the door of his home. He was willing to inconvenience his own life and schedule for the benefit of others. What might appear to be a sacrifice was a great blessing. It was no drudgery because his heart was right. He opened his home and used his resources because he had a desire to serve those who were serving others. You might be surprised what you could do for God if you would open your heart more to the work of God. You might be surprised how much you could do. I wonder, had he not opened his heart, would he have ever seen the opportunity he had within his home to be a blessing? Remember, we do not need lots of wealth and resources to be a blessing. All we need to do is open the door of our heart, and then God will show us what other doors we have to open.

"Down-to-Earth"

3 John 6 – "Which have borne witness of thy charity before the church: whom if thou bring forward on their journey after a godly sort, thou shalt do well:"

The name Gaius means "of the earth." He was no doubt an ordinary man with a heart to serve the Lord. His testimony can be seen in our verse for today. The Bible says that the brethren had spoken highly of his charity before the church. He was known to be a down-to-earth kind of man. I think this is a testimony that every believer should have.

The family of God has no place for high-minded, snooty, proud believers who think they are a cut above others. Gaius was a man who sought no glory and desired no praise. His charity was genuine, and he needed no recognition. However, he received the highest recognition a man could ever achieve in this life. His testimony is recorded in God's Word for all generations to read and to know. This is how God intended it to be. He praises those who seek no glory for themselves. He lifts people up who are down-to-earth and noble to His cause.

It is understandable how the world can be so lifted up in pride and develop "status" in society. What is disturbing is how easily it can filter into our churches. It is foolish to think that we are better than anyone in the church, or that we deserve a position more than anyone else does. We don't even deserve to be saved, let alone being allowed to serve. Many seek titles and trophies for their service. They look down on other people, thinking that they themselves are better than they are. Believers should never seek alliances with cliques that take hold in their local assembly, nor should they begin one by selectively picking other members whom they believe share their opinions and mindsets. This kind of attitude grieves the Spirit in the services. We will do well to remember that underneath the fancy clothes, titles, and compliments that we receive, we are nothing more than dust. May no accolades or accomplishments on this earth ever cause us to rise above it. We must stay in the dust where we belong. We must be down-to-earth.

"The Life of a Preacher"

3 John 7 – "Because that for his name's sake they went forth, taking nothing of the Gentiles."

We could say many things about our topic in today's devotional, but our verse gives us one thing in particular. The preachers who passed through the home of Gaius greatly enjoyed his fellowship and hospitality. He had refreshed them on their journey and encouraged them to keep traveling.

He witnessed firsthand what the life of a preacher is all about. It is a life of living by faith. While this is true for all believers, we must keep in mind that our verse is dealing primarily with how daily provisions are being met. These brethren had abandoned any attachments to monetary income for His name's sake. They were not looking to a Gentile world to supply their daily needs but were busy preaching the gospel and trusting God to supply. Gaius understood their commitment to the cause of Christ, and he was being used by God to help preachers.

I've had the privilege of spending time with preachers in my travels. I have seen a lot, having been in their homes and preached in their churches. Some preachers have been well taken care of by their church, and others have struggled greatly. I understand a lot can be factored in on both sides as to why or why not. However, when men forsake careers and good job opportunities to faithfully preach the Word, they should be cared for by the congregation. My philosophy is that you can never be too good to the man of God. He will never get rich serving the Lord. As preachers, we are not to worry about our financial future or to be greedy of gain. The life of a preacher is knowing that God signs your paycheck but you never know who He may use to deliver it to you. Remember, when the offering plate is passed for a missionary or evangelist, they are not seeking the world to aid them; they are living by faith.

"Helping the Preacher"

3 John 8 – *"We therefore ought to receive such, that we might be fellowhelpers to the truth."*

John says that we ought to contribute to men of God when they pass by our way; so that we can be fellow helpers in the ministry. I want to share some reasons in this verse why it is so important to help the preacher.

First, some will not receive them. The command is given to receive the preacher, but many will not obey the Scriptures. Some people and churches will not help meet their needs. A slap on the back or a "God bless you, brother" may be encouraging, but it does not put food on the table or gas in the tank. Receiving men of God is more than word and tongue; it requires action.

Second, they need our help. The Bible encourages us to be fellow helpers because preachers cannot carry the Gospel as effectively without our help. Everyone cannot go to Africa, China, or India. Everyone cannot travel the countryside preaching in churches week after week. Everyone can give, so that others can continue to carry on the work that God has called them to do.

Finally, we should help the preacher because it is an opportunity for us to be a partner and to be involved. Let me close this thought by saying that we should help preachers through the local church and under the leadership of the pastor and deacons. We should give our tithes and mission offerings faithfully and pray for the pastor and deacons to know who to help and when. As much as we may want to help everyone, we know in reality we cannot. God gives wisdom to those in leadership to know how to distribute according to the need. They will decide based on discernment and not emotions. We must remember that preachers need our help more now than ever.

"Do You Know This Man?"

3 John 9 – *"I wrote unto the church: but Diotrephes, who loveth to have the preeminence among them, receiveth us not."*

John has several things to say in this verse. First, he had written unto the church before but his letter was intercepted or hindered by a certain member. He also reveals who that member was by calling his name out in the text. I believe this is what should happen anytime someone tries to hinder the man of God from doing the Lord's work. They should immediately be called out so everyone will know of their evil deeds. He goes on to say that this man's problem was that he loved to have preeminence. Diotrephes wanted to run the show and would not receive the apostle, even though Christ had accepted John and had given him His approval in the ministry. Diotrephes still refused to receive him because he had an ulterior motive. My question to you is, "Have you ever met this man?"

I ask this question because I wish more members were wise to the undermining and manipulative games that some people play in church. A pastor has to keep a watchful eye to keep the church in check so that the flesh doesn't rule. In a day when people like to shine and be recognized, this can become a difficult task. Some pass through the church looking only for titles and trophies. If you give them a position or elevate them to a certain status in the church, they will be satisfied. It is not servitude that drives them; it is self-seeking glory. The problem with these types of people is that they can never be truly satisfied until they are number one.

Mark them because they are dangerous. Do not follow them or be fooled by their charisma or personality. If they are loving to everyone else in the church but are distant toward the man of God or his family, this should be a major red flag. They are exhibiting the same characteristic as this man in our text. I ask you again to think very carefully, "Do you know this man?"

"Dealing with Diotrephes"

3 John 10 – *"Wherefore, if I come, I will remember his deeds which he doeth, prating against us with malicious words: and not content therewith, neither doth he himself receive the brethren, and forbiddeth them that would, and casteth them out of the church."*

The apostle makes it clear that if he is able to come, then he will deal with Diotrephes. He also put it in writing and sent it with Gaius for all to hear in case he was unable to come. Either way, John makes it clear that these types of members cannot rule in the church. They must be dealt with and put in a position to either repent and get in line or be removed from the church.

The word "prating" means "to talk nonsense." He would say anything to slander those who go against him. He would not get along with anyone who would not go along with him. If you were not willing to bow at his feet, then he would destroy you with malicious words. He rejected the preacher in verse nine and the brethren in verse ten.

As a pastor, I have seen men and women come into the church like this man. They would first get a little following around the restaurant table after church services. Then they would build themselves up and try to minister to members that they could pull in around them. Finally, they would distance themselves from anyone loyal to the authority within the church. If they cannot be the authority, their goal is to undermine and reject the authority that is in place.

The man of God has to be careful and prayerful in dealing with a member like this. He must wait for either God to remove them or the right time to deal with them. A pastor's ultimate goal is to salvage them, but often they are too full of pride to repent. John knew that this man would have to be dealt with, and a real man of God knows that as well. Never allow yourself to be pulled into the wicked web of deceit by people like Diotrephes.

"Whom Will You Follow?"

3 John 11 – *"Beloved, follow not that which is evil, but that which is good. He that doeth good is of God: but he that doeth evil hath not seen God."*

Today's verse causes us to reflect on what we have read thus far in this Epistle. Diotrephes had done evil. Gaius had done good. We know that Gaius is of God because he loved and walked in the truth. Diotrephes had no vision of God. He is standing against everything that God is standing for. He is against the preacher, the brethren, and anyone who does not support his agenda.

John gives us another verse of warning not to follow this evil path. You might think that you would never go that way. I want to remind you that it has happened to the best of God's children. Do not ever get so wrapped up in another member of the church that you are blinded by their ways. To stay an arm's length of each other is a respectable distance. It allows us to be close, but not so close that we lose our focus.

Diotrephes must have had some influence. This means he probably was a likable person with a good personality. He probably knew what to say and when to say it to flatter people. He purposely tried to build a coalition in the church against the apostle.

It raises the question: Was he saved? Did he even know God? John says he that doeth evil hath not seen God. I'm about to make a statement that some may not agree with. I believe it to be true but you will have to draw your own conclusion. I know a child of God can get crossed up with the church or the preacher. However, those who are known for causing trouble repeatedly in a church and never repent or reap the consequences of the divisions they have caused, are not saved. The reason they seemingly "get by" with it is because they are lost. One day they will face God in judgment. John warns us not to be fooled by them.

"Having a Good Report"

3 John 12 – *"Demetrius hath good report of all men, and of the truth itself: yea, and we also bear record; and ye know that our record is true."*

The brother in our verse was responsible for carrying and delivering this Epistle. He had a good report with all of the churches and was endorsed by the apostle John. The Bible does not give us a lot of information about Demetrius, but it gives us enough to have great respect for him. This man is forever recorded in the pages of God's Word as having a good report with ALL men.

You see, many great men of the Bible did not have a good report with all men. Abraham was a man of great faith, but in Egypt, he was the man who lied about his wife. David was known as a great warrior, the sweet psalmist, the great king, and sadly, the great adulterer. Peter was the powerful preacher at Pentecost, but he was also the one who denied Jesus.

We understand that none of us are perfect and that all of our lives are flawed with mistakes. However, to be remembered as having a good report with all men is nothing to be overlooked. First and foremost, we should seek to please our Father in all that we do here on earth. We should also strive to keep our testimony right with others as well. What people say about us is not everything and in some cases not even true. At the same time, what men say about us is important.

Whenever I think about the word "report," I think about a document that tells the full story. A report is an update of where you are at the present time. It's not what one or two people report about you that tells the complete story, but what is said about you all across the pages of your life. What do most of your co-workers say about you? What is your report among your family as a whole? How does the church view you as a member? Do you have a good report? If your report is not what it should be, then seek to change it.

"So Much to Say"

3 John 13 – *"I had many things to write, but I will not with ink and pen write unto thee:"*

Whenever I read this verse, I am curious about the phrase "many things." John has written about many things in his Epistles, but in this third and final Epistle, he tells us he has so much more to say. I would love to know what more was on the great apostle's heart. What more did he have to write unto them? How much more detail or doctrine did he want to add? It leaves us wondering, but it also leaves us with a tremendous thought.

A man can spend his life teaching, preaching, and sharing the truths of God's Word, but when he gets to the final stretch of life, he realizes the half has not been told. There is still so much more to say about the Creator, the Christ, the Cross, the Comforter, the church, and the coming King and kingdom. We simply cannot get it all told!

As long as this world lasts, there will be more songs sung, more sermons preached, more books written, and more testimonies given about God, His Book, and His Son. It is a story that is never-ending, and the burden to share it never leaves. We simply pass it on to another generation so they can continue the work of declaring the message that John spoke of in the first chapter of the first Epistle.

John knew he could continue writing, but he felt inspired to wait and share his final thoughts when he came to see the brethren. Like John of old, we will all one day write our final words in life. We will lay down the pen of life, never to write in this world again. However, this does not mean we have nothing else to say; it just means we have run life's final race. As we cross the finish line from this world into the glory world, we will have so much more to say!

"Face to Face"

3 John 14 – "But I trust I shall shortly see thee, and we shall speak face to face. Peace be to thee. Our friends salute thee. Greet the friends by name."

John is giving his benediction with the mindset that he will come to see the brethren soon. He would rather say some things face-to-face instead of putting them in a letter. In this modern world of technology, some things are too personal and important to put in a text or an email. A phone call does not even seem sufficient. They bear more weight, demand more attention, and need to be said face-to-face. John felt this way, and I believe we should also be more sensitive about how we convey messages to individuals. There are times when what needs to be said must be said face-to-face.

When reading this verse, I can't get it off my heart that these are the final words and thoughts of the apostle. He uses terminology that not only makes me think in an earthly realm, but also in a heavenly realm. Spirit-filled saints will also provoke us to think beyond the temporary and into the eternal.

To further explain my thoughts, I think of the phrase "I shall shortly see thee." Even though I have never met this patriarch, I know that one day soon I shall shortly see him. This makes the Epistle personal to me. I feel a connection that I will see him along with so many others.

We will one day speak "face to face!" Can you imagine being face to face with family, friends, Christians of all ages, and most of all our Savior? Paul, Peter, James, John, Moody, Spurgeon, Mueller, and many more! We will live forever in a land of peace, and we will greet all of the brethren by name, just as he mentions in our verse. Heaven will be as personal as this verse we are reading. Allow me to close this devotional series, along with the apostle John in this verse, by saying to every reader who has taken the time to read these devotionals, "Our friends salute thee."

NOTES:

NOTES:

NOTES:

NOTES:

NOTES: